the BARISTA'S BIBLE

Olga Carryer

GINGKO PRESS

CONTENTS

INTRODUCTION 4

GETTING STARTED 8

—

COFFEE ART 28

COFFEE DRINKS 40

ALCOHOLIC DRINKS 74

COFFEE COOKIES 98

COFFEE CUPCAKES 128

COFFEE CAKES 170

—

INDEX 190

INTRODUCTION

Coffee is one of the most traded commodities in the world. It is grown in more than 50 countries, and for many their economies depend on it.

In this book we show you how to become a 'coffee artist', and present a definitive collection of fabulous recipes for coffee-based cakes and bakes.

The process of preparing and serving espresso-related beverages may seem a relatively simple task. However, as you start to use your espresso machine you may find that their production requires a good deal of practice.

You may notice that we refer to *'crema'* in the instructions. You may ask yourself, what's that?

Crema (or *schiuma* in Italian) is the creamy, golden brown extraction that develops in the filter holder and settles at the top of your espresso serving. Delicate oils in the espresso grind form colloids (very fine gelatin-like particles with a very slow rate of sedimentation). *Crema* is evidence that the correct amount of fresh coffee was ground to the proper consistency, and the precise amount of water at the correct temperature was quickly forced under pressure through the fine espresso grind.

THE HISTORY
OF COFFEE

According to a mythical tale, back in the 9th century, Kaldi, a humble Ethiopian goat-herd observed how his goats danced and pranced about after eating the red berries of a plant that we now know as the coffee plant. Amazed by the excitable behaviour of his herd, Kaldi collected some of the magical berries and consulted a holy man who cast them into a fire. The aroma produced by the roasting beans was so intoxicating that they were quickly retrieved, ground up and infused into hot water: history's first cup of hot coffee!

Coffee came to Italy from the Ottoman Empire during its thriving trade with Venice in the middle of the 17th century and the inaugural Venetian coffee house opened its doors in 1645. It took an Italian to establish the first café in Paris where, over mugs of hot coffee, Voltaire, Rousseau and Diderot developed the philosophies that would lead to the French Enlightenment.

Coffee houses soon spread across Europe and became a focal point of social interaction.

By 1901, the first espresso machine was patented. It forced boiling water and steam through ground coffee and into a cup. Unfortunately, the extreme heat of the water gave the coffee a burnt flavour. By World War II, piston machines replaced steam to make the coffee and kept the water at the optimal temperature. Because a lever was pulled to produce the coffee, it was colloquially called 'pulling a shot'.

By the 1960s, pump-driven machines replaced manual pistons and became standard in espresso bars.

Coffee drinking took on an entirely new face in the 1970s and '80s with the explosion of franchised coffee bar chains. Such bars prided themselves on high-quality beans and superior equipment to produce an excellent standard of coffee.

By the 1990s, consumer espresso machines brought café-quality coffee into the home. Such machines sported a high-voltage pump that generated excellent crema and a wand for steaming and frothing milk, making it possible for consumers to produce a cup of espresso of equal quality to those made by commercial machines.

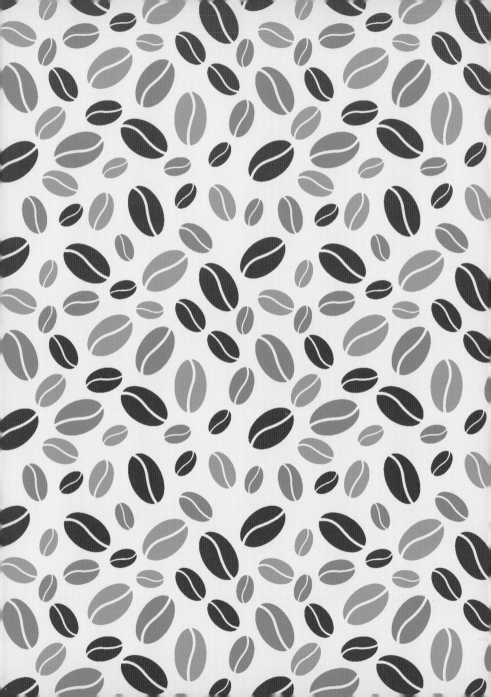

GETTING STARTED

CREATING THE PERFECT ESPRESSO

'Espresso' has become shorthand for caffè espresso, the beverage produced by forcing very hot water through finely ground coffee under force. It is this process that creates the elusive crema – the intense, silky layer of orange-brown foam that is the signature of an espresso coffee.

It is said that making the perfect cup of espresso requires four 'M's:

- Miscela (The Coffee Blend),
- Macinazione (Grinding the Beans),
- Macchina (The Espresso Machine), and
- Mano (The Skills of the Barista).

MISCELA — THE COFFEE BLEND

Coffee beans are chosen for a number of reasons: to create a signature blend, to balance the aromatics of different coffee species or to capture the purity of coffee from a particular coffee-growing region.

Arabica or Robusta — What's the Difference?

The two most important species of coffee plant used in coffee production are *arabica* and *robusta*. Originally indigenous to the mountains of Yemen, *Arabica* accounts for roughly two-thirds of the world's coffee production. It is also produced in the southwestern highlands of Ethiopia and southeastern Sudan, throughout Latin America, India, and to some extent in Indonesia.

Arabica's preference for higher altitudes has earned it the name 'mountain coffee'. *Arabica* beans produce a complex coffee taste of superior quality to the *robusta*, which is why many coffee blends will boast their beans are '100 per cent *Arabica*'.

Robusta, a variation of the species *Coffea canephora*, accounts for roughly a third of the coffee produced worldwide. It is cheaper to grow since it thrives at lower altitudes. *Robusta* is produced in West and Central Africa, Brazil and South-East Asia, particularly Vietnam. It contains more than twice the caffeine content of *arabica* beans, making it is more resistant to pests. *Robusta* tends to produce a brew that is more bitter than *arabica*, and imparts an earthy, even musty, flavour.

However, before you decide to reject *robusta*, you should know that only the lower grade *robusta* winds up as freeze-dried instant coffee, whereas the premium *robusta* crop is still used in espresso coffee blends. Coffee shops may use *arabica* as their primary bean but, because it is more expensive to grow, a blend containing some *robusta* makes the *arabica* more affordable.

Many Italian purveyors use 10 per cent *robusta* in their blends because it improves the consistency of crema.

In France, where they enjoy its bitter taste, the ratio of *robusta* to *arabica* can be as high as 45:55.

Most coffee drinkers are used to the taste of *robusta* from the supermarket aisle. Therefore you may find you enjoy the bitter edge and body of the *robusta* beans to the mellower taste of *arabica*.

Coffee Roasting

The roasting process forces moisture out of the bean and brings volatile oils to the surface of the bean. The essence of the espresso flavour is in these delicate oils. The darker the roast, the longer the bean has been roasted, and a dark roast can have less caffeine than a lighter roast. As the heat of the roaster forces moisture out of the bean, the bean expands but the weight, because of the extraction of moisture, diminishes.

There is no precise standardized terminology used to describe the coffee roast. Viennese, Italian, French and American are not the origin of the bean, but instead refer to the degree of roasting, and that depends on the standards of the roaster.

Finding the Right Blends

If you choose to experiment with the best espresso blend for your taste, look first at those offered by boutique coffee roasters. There are countless purveyors of fine coffee who select choice green beans, which they roast themselves and then combine into a range of different blends. Many of these roasters have an online presence where you can order excellent whole or ground coffee blends. Some even offer sample packs for tasting to enable you to choose a blend that suits you. Others allow you to make your own blend of different regional coffees.

Coffee contains 800 different aromatic compounds, including hints of chocolate and smoky, cigar-like aftertones, and these boutique roasters have spent years perfecting different blends for a range of tastes, occasions and ethical concerns.

Organic

For coffee to be certified organic, it means that no chemicals or pesticides were used on the farm or during processing in the producing country of origin.

Decaffeinated

The 'hit' that coffee-drinkers perceive they get from a sip of a good cup of coffee is often nothing to do with caffeine, but rather from the intense flavour. Good decaffeinated coffee can still offer that flavour hit but without the caffeine.

Decaffeination is usually carried out by the Swiss water method pioneered by the Swiss Water Decaffeinated Coffee Company in the 1930s. Raw green coffee beans are soaked in hot water to release the caffeine and the beans discarded. The remaining water passes through a carbon filter that traps the caffeine but preserves the coffee solids. The resulting extract is used to capture caffeine from new green beans added to it, creating raw beans that are 99.9 per cent caffeine-free. The caffeine is lost but not the flavour.

Those simply wanting to reduce their caffeine, not eliminate it entirely, might confine themselves to 100 per cent *arabica* beans only since these contain about half the caffeine of *robusta*.

Fair Trade Certified

Much of the world's coffee crop is grown in developing countries. In recent years, it has become possible to support these producers better by purchasing fair trade certified coffee. This means that the coffee is bought directly from the farmers and growers at a fair price, rather than via conventional trade economics that discriminates against the poorest and weakest producers. A fair trade partnership helps to improve local sustainability and quality of life in these impoverished areas by channelling money into important community infrastructure such as schools and hospitals.

Rainforest Alliance Certified

The Rainforest Alliance is an international non-profit organisation dedicated to the conservation of tropical forests that works to conserve biodiversity by transforming land-use and business practices to ensure sustainable livelihoods. Coffee that is Rainforest Alliance Certified (RFA) is derived from farms and forests where water, soil and wildlife habitat are conserved, where workers are treated well, and where families have access to education and health care. So both coffee consumers and the communities where coffee is produced benefit.

MACINAZIONE — GRINDING THE BEANS

As anyone who has ever sniffed freshly ground coffee beans will know, the flavour of the coffee is at its best immediately after the beans are ground.

In fact, the most discerning baristas will only grind beans for espresso directly before using them. Coffee puritans swear that it only takes 30 seconds in the open air for ground beans to become too stale for a good espresso. It is true that ground beans slowly lose their flavour over time, but this can be reduced if the coffee is properly stored.

How to Store Coffee

If you purchase your coffee already ground, remember that it is highly perishable since so much more surface area is exposed to the air, which robs its flavour. Because of this, coffee is often vacuum packed, which keeps the beans fresh for only a few weeks. Be warned that many packaged, imported coffees are already months old before they reach the supermarket shelves.

It is best, therefore, to grind coffee beans yourself of buy your coffee fresh each week. If this is not practical, buy the smallest quantity you can manage, and store it in an airtight, moisture-proof container in a cool place. A glass or ceramic container with a rubber seal is ideal. Do NOT store coffee in the refrigerator or freezer. When cold coffee is brought into room temperature, a layer of water condenses on its surface which damages the aromatic flavour oils. Like tea, coffee attracts and absorbs foreign odours, so protect your coffee from contamination from other foodstuffs that can affect the flavour.

Which Grinder?

We all know there is no contest between ground coffee and the coffee you grind yourself. Also, whole beans keep far longer than ground, so obtaining whole beans and grinding just before brewing is ideal. There are two main varieties of home coffee grinders – blade grinders and burr grinders.

Blade Grinders

These operate like a small home blender by using fast-moving blades to chop the beans. The grind produced by such machines varies from chunks to fine powder. This inconsistent grind is okay for stove-top or drip coffee makers, but not for pump- or piston-driven espresso machines that require a uniformly fine grind. Such grinders also heat the beans, which can tamper with the flavour profile of the coffee.

Burr Grinders

Using a burr grinder will give homogenous grinding so the particle size of the coffee is consistent and even, which is especially important for espresso. If the particle size of the coffee is uniform, equal amounts of the coffee's profile will be extracted. However, if the particle size of the coffee varies, some particles will be over-extracted and some will be under-extracted, resulting in poor tasting coffee.

These grinders may be either electric or operated by hand. They contain corrugated steel burrs that rotate to shave the beans. The benefit of such machines is that may be adjusted to achieve different grinds and they also minimise heat production that can affect the flavour of the coffee.

Before investing in a home grinder, consider how much you wish to spend and how much time you are prepared to devote to use and maintenance. Manual burr grinders are cheaper but require some elbow grease to operate. The more expensive the electric machine, the greater degree of grind adjustment available, which is preferable. The correct grind is a vital step in preparing café-quality espresso — this may require a period of trial and error to fine-tune the consistency of the grind to your particular espresso machine. A grinder that does not achieve the exact grind you require for your coffee machine type will be a waste of money.

Some modern electric burr grinders include electronic sensors for precision grinding and a portion-control container that measures out the precise amount of coffee required each time. Certainly the cost of a burr grinder is worth the investment, because whole beans retain their freshness longer than ground coffee, and you can adjust the grind to suit your machine to obtain that perfect cup of espresso.

Like any equipment used to prepare food, grinders require maintenance and cleaning to be kept in optimal condition. There is little point grinding freshly roasted beans in a machine that contains old coffee residue that has turned rancid.

Which Grind?

Plunger	: Medium Fine
Filter/Drip Method	: Fine
Espresso And Stovetop	: Very Fine
Greek And Turkish	: Powder

Whether grinding coffee yourself or buying it ready ground, ensure the grind is appropriate for your machine.

The grind determines how fast the coffee flavour is extracted. Too coarse a grind will produce watery coffee. Too fine a grind will over-extract the coffee and make it bitter.

Also, the grind has to be uniform in order to ensure the best taste. Generally speaking, the faster the brewing method, the finer the grind required.

For your espresso machine, the beans must be ground fine, but not too fine. If the grind is too fine – a powder grind – water cannot flow through the grind even under pressure. A powder grind feels like flour when rubbed between the fingers. A fine grind should feel gritty, like salt.If the water flows too slowly or not at all, the grind is too fine for your machine.

Another variable is the quality of the coffee used and the pressure applied when tamping the coffee in the coffee basket. A more powerful machine develops greater pressure and therefore takes a finer grind. However, if the grind is too fine, or the coffee tamped too compactly, the water under pressure in the brew head will not be able to flow through the grind and coffee may spurt from around the filter holder.

The proper grind for your particular machine is critical to extracting a crema espresso. You will need to test the fineness of the grind at different indexes on the grinder before determining the optimum grind for your machine.

If you are desperate, you can pulverise the roasted beans using a mortar and pestle, but this generally reduces the bean to the power consistency required for Greek or Turkish coffee and is too fine for espresso.

MACCHINA — THE ESPRESSO MACHINE

To bring the café experience into your kitchen, what you need is a piston-lever or pump-driven machine that generates sufficient pump pressure to force hot water through the fine coffee grind.

Electric, non-pump machines are the highest selling coffee machines for the home market today. These entry-level machines are cheaper than their pump counterparts, but will still produce a serviceable long black. However, non-pump machines rely on steam pressure and so do not provide the 'grunt' for creating café-quality crema, which is the basis for many coffee beverages as well as the prerequisite for producing coffee art in the home.

Espresso machine pressure is measured in atmospheres (atm) or pounds per square inch (psi). Non-pump machines only generate pressure to an average of 3 atm or 44 psi. Pump-driven machine, on the other hand, achieve pressures of up to 9–17 atm or 135–250 psi.

The latest technology in the home espresso machine is the thermoblock system, which replaces the boiler with a thermal block. Because the water is flash-heated by the thermoblock, steam is continuously available for frothing or steaming milk (while there is still water in the reservoir).

If you are wanting to improve your skills as a barista and experiment with coffee art, you require at least a pump-driven or piston-lever machine. However, if ease of operation is more important, there are also automatic machines that complete the whole ritual of coffee making for you, with programs for different coffee types at the click of a button. Espresso machines are also available in combination with ordinary drip models for households that require espresso drinkers and drip-coffee drinkers to be catered for by a single unit.

MANO — THE SKILLS OF THE BARISTA

Even with a state-of-the-art espresso machine, the quality of the coffee still relies on the talent of the barista.

As 'mano' is the Italian word for hand, this final 'M' refers to the talents of the barista. 'Barista' is the Italian word for bartender, although it has come to refer specifically to a person skilled in the art of coffee making.

Even if you have purchased a state-of-the-art espresso machine, making coffee still requires practice. The most important thing is to know your equipment, including the grinder and the espresso machine. Be sure to read the manual that comes with the machine. Thankfully, home espresso machines today require less skill, but the espresso maker is still a sophisticated piece of equipment that requires some initial self-training to use. For example, you need to know how to fill your filter basket properly, how to tamp the ground coffee, the best movements required for frothing the milk.

Like all skills, making the perfect espresso requires practice. There is no rewind switch or undo button when making a cup of coffee, so achieving the perfect crema beings with some trial and error. But, don't take it too seriously – learning to become a home barista is part of the fun of owning your machine. With patience, you will eventually learn to pull every shot with the beautiful crema that is the mark of true espresso.

—

TO MAKE GREAT COFFEE WITH YOUR COFFEE MACHINE, ALWAYS FOLLOW THE 5 BASIC STEPS...

1. EMPTY OLD COFFEE GROUNDS THOROUGHLY
2. RINSE OUT OLD GROUNDS
3. WIPE THE HANDLE
4. PACK THE COFFEE GENTLY
5. TAMP WITH REASONABLE PRESSURE (NOT TOO HARD)

—

Coffee Art

If making coffee is a science – from the roasting and grinding of the beans to the perfect brewing temperature to extract the ultimate coffee flavour – then creating unique images on the coffee surface is an art.

Coffee art or latte art requires a perfect combination of crema and steamed milk foam. The milk is steamed using the wand on the espresso machine until the stainless steel jug feels too hot to touch but not boiling. The resulting froth – sometimes called microfoam – has a smooth, meringue-like texture.

The secret to creating the coffee art canvas is in the pour. The milk should be poured at a consistent rate into the centre of the espresso so that the milk disappears under the brown layer of crema or is layered on, depending on the design you wish to achieve. A teaspoon and other tools are used to add final droplets of milk foam, which are then manipulated against the brown base to create interesting designs. You will be amazed at the array of patterns you can create with a skewer or a teaspoon, from seagulls and hearts, to flowers and leaves, and even smiley faces!

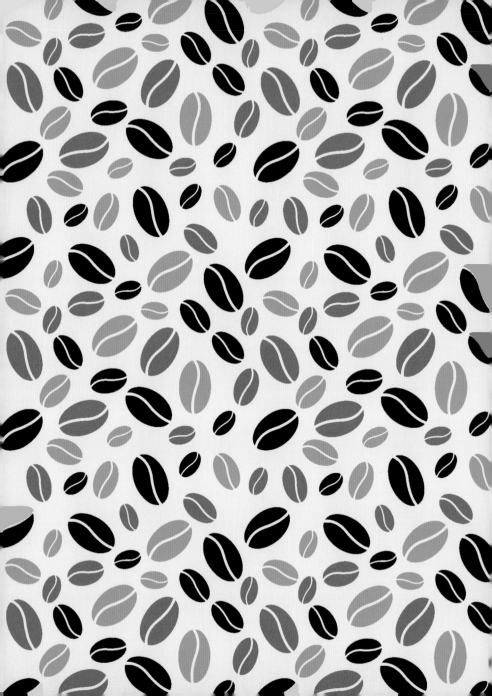

COFFEE
ART

—

A LOT OF CARE NEEDS TO BE
TAKEN WHEN POURING THE
MILK FOR COFFEE ART SO YOU
DON'T DESTROY THE CREMA.
SPOONS, COCKTAIL STICKS AND
OTHER POINTED UTENSILS MAY
BE USED TOGETHER WITH A
GOOD POURING JUG TO PLACE
THE FROTH ON THE COFFEE AND
CREATE THE DESIRED DESIGN.

—

FREE-POURED PATTERNS

Free-poured patterns are used to create hearts, rosettas, apples, tulips, sparrows and other designs in the milk on top of the coffee.

Most are created by moving the milk jug (pitcher) a certain way when pouring. Don't be disappointed if you can't get these patterns correct immediately as they require practice. Ultimately, you will need perfect shots and perfect milk every time in order to make these designs.

Pouring the Milk

Hold the cup on its ear and slightly at an angle. Start pouring the milk slowly into the crema. You do not want to pour too slowly, as this will leave the foam behind in the jug. You also do not want to pour too quickly because this will break the crema apart. Pour slowly in a few spots in the cup to break through the crema.

Start pouring the milk into the back of the cup once the cup seems just more than half full. Now slowly but very steadily move the pitcher from side to side. This is a wrist movement and should be done just slightly. The milk should not swing from side to side in the jug. Keep moving it from side to side in one spot in the cup until you see the foam appearing. If you see distinct white lines forming, you're on the right track. Once you see the foam break through the crema you can start pouring patterns. Keep practising and eventually you will be rewarded with your own latte design.

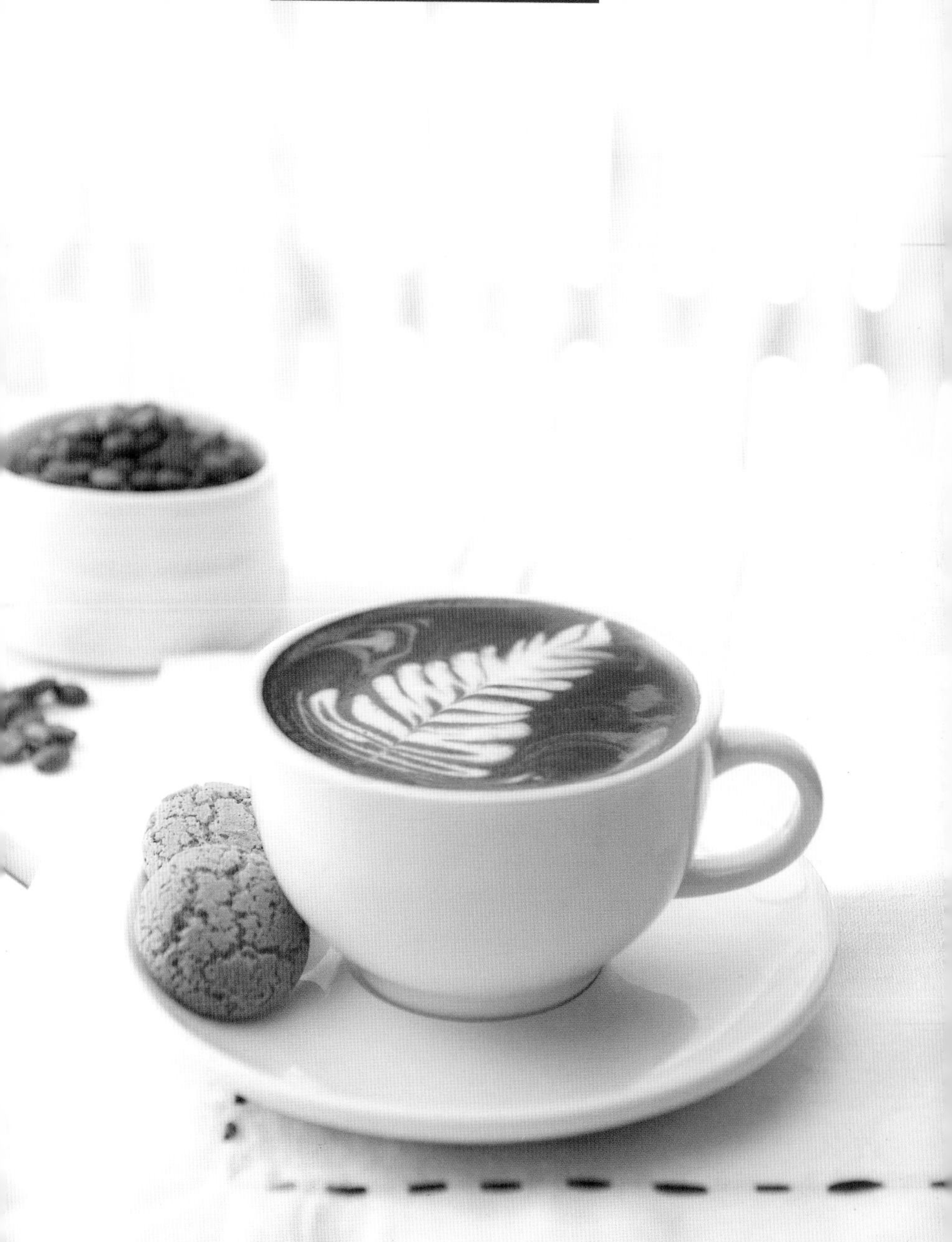

HEART

Pour slowly in the middle to settle the crema to form a base to work with. About halfway through, start tilting the jug forward to release some froth.

Continue pouring into the middle and let the white circle form.

Near the top of the cup start tilting the jug back upwards and move to the other side of the cup in a scooping motion.

ROSETTA

Pour slowly to settle the crema to create a good base.
This allows the milk to separate to form the pattern.

About halfway through pouring, move the jug from
side to side until you see the foam appearing on the surface.
Keep moving the jug from side to side until you see curved
white lines appear. Now slowly move the jug backwards
while still moving it from side to side.

Once you have reached the edge of the cup, start
tilting the jug back upwards and move back down the
centre of the leaves in a scooping motion.

Note:
Quick movements
from side to side
will create a rosetta
with lots of leaves.
Slow movements
from side to side
will create fewer
and thicker leaves.

PATTERNS WITH CHOCOLATE

The easiest way to make coffee art is to use chocolate syrup to form the design. This is because the finished product is not dependent on the way the coffee is poured. However, it is always good practice to keep as much of the crema on the coffee as possible.

Use a good brand of chocolate powder and mix it with boiling water to form a chocolate paste that sits well on the coffee. Make sure the powder is well mixed and there are no clumps.

An even better option is to use espresso shots to mix the chocolate instead of the boiling water – you will find that the resulting flavour is far superior.

Use a clean squeezy bottle to decant the sauce into and ensure it has a good nozzle. Alternatively, pour the sauce into the corner of a clear plastic bag and clip off the corner. Twist the excess bag out of the way and use the filled corner like a piping bag.

Note:
Chocolate etching should only be placed on cappuccinos, hot chocolates and mochas.

Chocolate Sauce

To a 30 ml (1 fl oz) espresso shot add 60 ml (1/4 cup) of powdered chocolate and mix thoroughly. The sauce should be thick and easy to work with. If it's too thin and watery, add more chocolate. If too thick, add a little more espresso.

SPIDER'S WEB

Pour your coffee.

Using a chocolate bottle, start squeezing chocolate sauce into the middle of the coffee. Make a spiral motion with your hand, until you reach the edge of the cup.

Using a clean skewer, and starting at the edge of the cup, drag it into the middle. Repeat this process several times around the cup, cleaning the skewer each time for a clean finish.

QUICK AND SIMPLE

Pour the coffee and use a spoon to cover it with white froth.
Using a chocolate sauce bottle, draw a random continuous
circle on the white base. The more circles, the more effective
the design.

Using a skewer, starting on the outside of the circles,
dip into the coffee and drag into the centre. Wipe your skewer
each time. Repeat this process several times, making your
way around the circle.

Note:
You can use a
brown base also
but white gives
more definition.

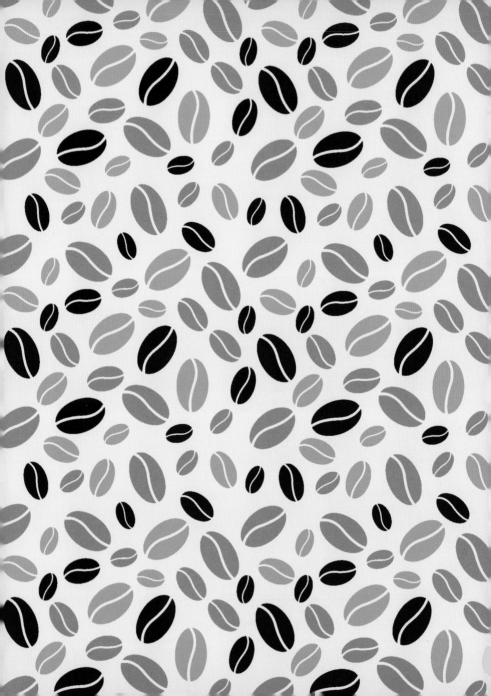

COFFEE
DRINKS

—

MANY PEOPLE DRINK COFFEE
IN ITS WELL-KNOWN VARIATIONS,
SUCH AS CAPPUCCINO, CAFFÈ LATTE,
FLAT WHITE, ESPRESSO, MACCHIATO,
AND LONG BLACK. HOWEVER,
THERE ARE MANY OTHER
SPECIALTY COFFEES AVAILABLE,
AND WE HAVE LISTED A NUMBER
OF THESE IN THIS CHAPTER.
DRINK ON AND ENJOY THE
WONDERFUL TASTES OF
BEAUTIFULLY BREWED COFFEE.

—

SHOT
VARIABLES

**The main variables in a shot of espresso are the size
and length. Terminology is standardized, but precise
sizes and proportions vary substantially. Cafés
generally have a standardized shot (size and length),
such as 'triple ristretto', only varying the number
of shots in espresso-based drinks such as lattes but
not changing the extraction – changing between
a double and a triple only requires changing the
filter basket size, while changing between ristretto,
normale, and lungo require changing the grind.**

Size

The size can be a single, double or triple, which correspond roughly
to a 30, 60 or 90 ml (1, 2 or 3 fl oz) standard (normale) shot, and use a
proportional amount of ground coffee, roughly 7–8, 14–16, and 21–24
grams (¼, ½, or ¾ oz); correspondingly sized filter baskets are used.
The single shot is the traditional shot size, being the maximum that
could easily be pulled on a lever machine, while the double is the
standard shot today.

Single baskets are sharply tapered or stepped down in diameter
to provide comparable depth to the double baskets and, therefore,
comparable resistance to water pressure.

In espresso-based drinks, particularly larger milk-based drinks,
a drink with three or four shots of espresso will be called a 'triple' or
'quad', respectively, but this does not mean that the shots themselves
are triple or quadruple shots.

Length

The length of the shot can be ristretto (restricted), normale/
standard (normal) or lungo (long): these correspond to a smaller
or larger drink with the same amount of ground coffee and same
level of extraction. Proportions vary, and the volume (and low
density) of crema make volume-based comparisons difficult
(precise measurement uses the mass of the drink), but proportions
of 1:1, 1:2 and 1:3–4 are common for ristretto, normale and lungo,
corresponding to 30, 60 and 90–120 ml/1, 2 and 3–4 fl oz) for a
double shot. Ristretto is the most commonly used of these terms,
and double or triple ristrettos are particularly associated with
artisan-type espresso.

Ristretto, normale and lungo are not simply the same shot,
stopped at different times – this will result in an under-extracted
shot (if run too short a time) or an over-extracted shot (if run
too long a time). Rather, the grind is adjusted (finer for ristretto,
coarser for lungo) so that the target volume is achieved by the
time extraction finishes.

ESPRESSO (SHORT BLACK)

Espresso is an Italian name for a coffee beverage. In Italy, the rise of espresso consumption coincided with urbanisation. Espresso bars provided a place to socialise and coffee prices were controlled by local authorities, provided the coffee was consumed standing up. This encouraged the 'stand at the bar' culture.

A true Italian espresso is 30 ml (1 fl oz) of beverage with a thick, golden crema on the surface. True espresso is a complex beverage, combining a special blend of arabica beans, darkly roasted, finely ground, densely packed and quickly brewed under pressure in individual servings. Properly brewed espresso with crema has a uniquely smooth and creamy bittersweet flavour that captures the full essence of the beans, a distinctive flavour not found in any other type of coffee.

1   Firmly tamp 1 tablespoon of ground coffee to ensure that the water flow is restricted. The pour/extraction should take about 15–20 seconds.

2   Serve in a small 90 ml (3 fl oz) ceramic glass or demitasse cup with a layer of golden crema on top.

> **Note:**
> The size of an espresso can be a single or 'solo' (30 ml/1 fl oz),
> double or 'doppio' (60 ml/2 fl oz), or triple or 'triplo' (90 ml/3 fl oz).
> The length of the shot can also be varied – ristretto (restricted),
> normale (normal) or lungo (long).

LONG BLACK / AMERICANO

Long black is a style of coffee most commonly found in Australia and New Zealand, but now becoming available in the UK. It's made by pulling a double shot of espresso over hot water (not boiling) – the hot water also comes from the espresso machine.

The order in which a long black is made is important. The espresso should be full bodied, with a good crema. A long black is made in a 160 ml (5½ fl oz) cup, using the proportions of 3 parts hot water to 2 parts espresso (2 shots)

A similar coffee is the Americano, which is made in reverse order to the long black – coffee first, water second.

This coffee originated during World War 2 when American girls overseas would pour hot water into espresso to try and make it like the coffee they were used to back home.

1   Pour 90 ml (3 fl oz) of hot water in a cup.

2   Firmly tamp 2 tablespoons of ground coffee to ensure that the water flow is restricted. Use a twin group head for an even extraction. The pour/extraction should take about 30–35 seconds.

3   Serve in a standard 160 ml (5½ fl oz) ceramic or glass cup with a layer of golden caramel crema.

MACCHIATO / LATTE MACCHIATO

'Macchiato' means marked or stained. Espresso macchiato is a single espresso 'stained' with a small amount (1–2 teaspoons) of hot or cold milk, usually with a small amount of foamed milk on top. The foamed milk was traditionally added to show the beverage had a little milk in it, so it wasn't confused with an espresso on serving. This coffee can also be served as a long macchiato, (a double espresso stained with a small amount of hot or cold milk). A macchiato is made in a 90 ml (3 fl oz) cup using 1 shot (30 ml/1 fl oz) espresso, 1–2 teaspoons of hot or cold milk.

Latte macchiato literally means 'stained milk'. It is a drink in which steamed white milk is 'stained' by the addition of espresso. Latte macchiato differs from a caffè latte in that the espresso is added to the milk, rather than the other way around; it features more foam, rather than just hot milk; only a half-shot or less of espresso is used; and the drink is usually layered, not mixed together.

....

1   Firmly tamp 1 tablespoon of ground coffee to ensure that the water flow is restricted. The pour/extraction should take about 15–20 seconds.

2   Serve in a 90 ml (3 fl oz) glass or ceramic cup with a layer of golden crema on top. Add a dash of cold milk before serving.

> **Note:**
> To make long macchiato, use 2 tablespoons of ground coffee and use a twin group head for an even extraction.

CAFFÈ LATTE

In Italy, the caffè latte is traditionally a breakfast drink, prepared at home. Outside of Italy it is a standard (30 ml/1 fl oz) or double (60 ml/2 fl oz) shot espresso, filled with steamed milk and a layer of foamed milk (approximately 12 mm/½ in) on top.

Caffè latte is an Italian term for a double serving of espresso with steamed milk. Café au lait in French, café con leche in Spanish and kaffee mit milch in German are the same thing.

The caffè latte serving is roughly one part espresso to two parts steamed milk, served in a 160 ml (5½ fl oz) wide-mouthed glass or ceramic cup. Lattes are also served embellished with flavourings added before the espresso, or steamed with the milk.

Caffè latte is similar to a cappuccino, the difference being that a cappuccino consists of espresso and steamed milk with a 2 cm (¾ in) layer of thick milk foam.

Another similar drink, which originated in Australia and New Zealand, is the flat white, which is served in a smaller ceramic cup with creamy steamed milk poured over a single shot of espresso, holding back the lighter froth on the top of the milk.

....

1   Firmly tamp 1 tablespoon of ground coffee.
     The pour should be 30 ml (1 fl oz) of coffee.

2   Add 60 ml (2 fl oz) hot milk. Scoop milk froth
     to the top of the glass.

Note: Create coffee art on top if you wish.

PICCOLO LATTE

Piccolo latte is a variant of caffè latte. It is a single espresso shot in a machiatto glass, which is then filled with steamed milk in the same fashion as a caffè latte. It is a 60 ml (2 fl oz) drink, with a 1:1 ratio of coffee to steamed milk, and about 5 mm (¼ in) of foam on the top.

1   Firmly tamp 1 tablespoon of ground coffee.
     Pour 30 ml (1 fl oz) coffee into the glass

2   Add 30 ml (1 fl oz) hot milk.

3   Scoop milk froth onto the top of the glass.

Note: Create coffee art on top if you wish.

FLAT WHITE

The flat white originated in Australia and New Zealand during the early 1980s. It is prepared by pouring steamed milk from the bottom of a steaming jug over a single shot of espresso.

The drink is typically served in 160 ml (5½ fl oz) ceramic cups. To achieve the flat, no-froth texture the steamed milk is poured from the bottom of the jug, holding back the lighter froth on top in order to access the milk with smaller bubbles, making the drink smooth and velvety in texture and keeping the crema intact.

1 Firmly tamp 1 tablespoon of ground coffee. Pour 30 ml (1 fl oz) espresso. The pour/extraction should take about 15–20 seconds.

2 Add 60 ml (2 fl oz) fresh hot milk.

Note: Create coffee art on top if you wish.

CAPPUCCINO

The origin of the word 'cappuccino' dates back more than 500 years to the Capuchin order of friars. The order's name derives from its long, pointed cowl or 'cappuccino', a derivative of 'cappuccio' meaning 'hood' in Italian. It is said that the coffee was named after the friars because the colour of the coffee resembled the colour of their habit. The first recorded use of the word cappuccino in English was in 1948.

It is made with one-third espresso, one-third milk and one-third creamy, heavy, dense foam (not light, bubbly, tasteless froth) and served in a 160 ml (5½ fl oz) ceramic cappuccino cup.

Steamed milk at the bottom of the frothing jug is poured over the espresso, and the froth on top of the jug is spooned on top to cap the cappuccino and retain the heat. Cappuccino is often garnished with a light dusting of chocolate or unsweetened cocoa powder, cinnamon, nutmeg, vanilla powder or coloured sugar crystals.

1 Firmly tamp 1 tablespoon of ground coffee. Pour 30 ml (1 fl oz) coffee into the cup. The pour/extraction should take about 15–20 seconds.

2 Add 30 ml (1 fl oz) fresh hot milk.

3 Add 30 ml (1 fl oz) milk froth, which can sit higher than the rim of the cup.

4 Dust with chocolate powder.

Note: Create coffee art on top if you wish.

MOCHA

The caffè mocha takes its name from the Red Sea coastal town of Mocha, Yemen, which as far back as the 15th century was a dominant exporter of coffee, especially to areas around the Arabian Peninsula.

A caffè mocha is a variant of a caffè latte. Like a latte, it is typically one part espresso and two parts steamed milk, but a portion of chocolate is added, typically in the form of drinking chocolate, although chocolate syrup is also used. Mochas may contain dark or milk chocolate.

Like cappuccino, mochas contain the well-known milk froth on top, although they are sometimes served with whipped cream instead. They are usually topped with a dusting of either cinnamon or cocoa powder. Marshmallows may also be added on top for flavour and decoration.

A variant is white caffè mocha, made with white chocolate instead of milk or dark. There are also variants of the drink that mix the two syrups – this mixture is referred to by several names, including black and white mocha, tan mocha, tuxedo mocha and zebra.

....

1   Pour one teaspoon of drinking chocolate into a 250 ml (8 fl oz) coffee cup.

2   Firmly tamp 1 tablespoon of ground coffee. Fill the cup one-third of the way with coffee.

3   Top with steamed milk. Dust with drinking chocolate powder.

Note: Create coffee art on top if you wish.

VIENNA COFFEE

Vienna coffee is a popular cream-based coffee. It is made by preparing strong shots of espresso into a standard cup or glass and topping with cream (instead of milk or sugar). The coffee is drunk through the cream top.

Legend has it that soldiers of the Polish-Habsburg army, while liberating Vienna from the second Turkish siege in 1683, came across a number of sacks of strange beans, which they first thought were camel feed and wanted to destroy. The Polish king granted the sacks to a Polish noble named Franz Georg Kolschitzky, who was instrumental in defeating the Turkish. He opened a coffee house called the Blue Bottle, and began serving coffee as it was prepared in Constantinople (a concoction of pulp and water). The Viennese did not take to this and, after experimentation, Kolschitzky decided to filter the coffee and add cream and honey. Success was immediate.

....

1 Firmly tamp 2 tablespoons of ground coffee to ensure that the water flow is restricted. Pour 2 shots or 60 ml (2 fl oz) hot coffee into the glass. The pour/extraction should take about 15–20 seconds.

2 Top with whipped cream and dust with unsweetened cocoa powder.

ICED COFFEE

Iced coffee can be a refreshing afternoon treat if it's really hot outside and you want to cool down but still have coffee.

There are many variations of iced coffee, depending on which country you are in. It may be served chilled with ice cream and/or whipped cream. It may be a frozen coffee-flavoured slushie mixed with cream, or it may be straight espresso kept in the freezer and served as a slushie. You could have strong black coffee sweetened with sugar, heavy cream and cardamom, quickly cooled and served over ice, or coffee with condensed milk poured over ice.

1 Firmly tamp 2 tablespoons of ground coffee to ensure that the water flow is restricted. Pour the coffee. The pour/ extraction should take about 15–20 seconds.

2 Transfer the hot coffee to a carafe or pitcher. Refrigerate until cold, about 2–3 hours.

3 Add 1 scoop of ice cream to a 400 ml (14 fl oz) milkshake glass.

4 Pour over one part cold coffee to one-third fill the glass.

5 Pour over two-parts cold milk to 1 cm (½ in) under the brim and stir.

6 Top with whipped or ice cream and decorate with cocoa powder and coffee beans.

ICED CHOCOLATE

Iced chocolate is a wonderful way to get a chocolate fix in hot weather
– when a hot chocolate just won't do!

A variation of this drink is the iced mocha, in which chilled coffee
is mixed into the chocolate, topped up with milk and served with ice
cream and/or whipped cream.

1   Mix 2 tablespoons of drinking chocolate with a little hot water
    or milk to make a smooth, thick liquid. Add a shot of coffee.

2   Drizzle the liquid decoratively around the inside of a tall 400 ml
    (14 fl oz) glass.

3   Add some ice.

4   Pour 250 ml (8 fl oz) cold milk to 1 cm (½ in) under the brim
    of the glass.

5   Top with whipped or ice cream and dust with chocolate powder.

HOT MOCHA CHOCOLATE

Hot chocolate is a heated beverage typically consisting of melted chocolate or cocoa powder and hot milk, served with or without sugar. Drinking chocolate is a commercial version.

The first chocolate beverage is believed to have been created by the Mayan people around 2000 years ago. The beverage became popular in Europe after being introduced from Mexico, though the drink we enjoy today would have been unrecognisable to the ancient peoples.

HOT CHOCOLATE

1 Mix 1 tablespoon of drinking chocolate in a mug with a little hot water or milk to make a smooth, thick liquid. Add a shot of coffee.

2 Fill the mug with hot frothed milk and dust with chocolate or add a swirl of chocolate syrup. Serve with marshmellows or mini-meringues.

ITALIAN HOT CHOCOLATE

1 Add 250 ml (8 fl oz) milk to a medium saucepan set over low heat. Whisk in 2 oz (60 g) of quality plain or milk chocolate chips until thoroughly incorporated and no lumps remain. Add a shot of coffee.

2 Stir in a hint of additional flavouring such as a drop of vanilla or almond extract or a teaspoon of Grand Marnier. Dust with cinnamon or nutmeg.

BABYCINO

A babycino (also known as a steamer) is a drink of frothed milk but no coffee. It is primarily marketed towards children. It can have flavoured syrups added, or be topped with chocolate sprinkles or marshmallows.

1 Drizzle coffee-flavoured syrup decoratively around the inside of a glass.

2 Fill with hot or warm frothed milk.

3 Add marshmallow if desired. Sprinkle with chocolate powder.

Favoured Syrups:
With the growth of speciality coffee in the early 1990s came an increased popularity in flavoured syrups, which are used to add other flavour notes to lattes and hot drinks. The range of flavours available continues to grow. Flavours are fun, easy to use, and offer endless ways to customize drinks.

Note:
When using flavoured syrup in a hot drink, make sure you add the syrup first, and extract your coffee into the syrup – this will activate the flavour component in the syrup and make sure it is evenly dispersed in the cup.

BANANA MOCHA MILKSHAKE

A delicious variation on the iced coffee that makes a perfect morning treat. Add Kahlúa for a decadent alcoholic twist.

1 Place 250 ml (8 fl oz) of milk, 150 g (5 oz) of sliced ripe banana, 2 tablespoons sugar and 30 ml (1 fl oz) of espresso in a blender and blend until smooth.

2 Freeze in the blender container for 1 hour, or until slightly frozen. Loosen the mixture from the sides of the blender container, add 50 ml (1 fl oz) of vanilla yogurt and blend until smooth. Serve immediately.

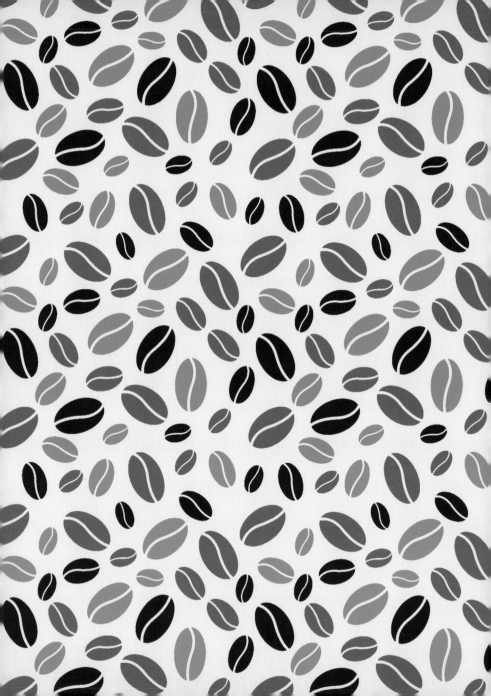

ALCOHOLIC
DRINKS

AFFOGATO AGAVE

makes 1

2 scoops vanilla ice cream
60 ml (2 fl oz)
  espresso coffee
2 tablespoons Patron XO
  Café Tequila, Frangelico
  or Kahlúa
1 teaspoon hazelnuts,
  chopped

1 Put the ice cream in the glass and drown
it with the espresso coffee.

2 Pour over your choice of liqueur.

3 Decorate with chopped hazelnuts.

CAFÉ AGAVE

makes 1

2 tablespoons Patron XO
   Café Tequila
2 tablespoons cocoa liqueur
60 ml (2 fl oz)
   espresso coffee
60 ml (2 fl oz) cream
chocolate flakes

1 Shake all the ingredients, except the chocolate flake, with ice and strain into the glass.

2 Serve in a martini glass, garnished with chocolate flakes.

CARIBBEAN COFFEE

makes 1

2 tablespoons dark rum
150 ml (¼ pint) hot
   black coffee
Sugar, to sweeten
3 tablespoons
   whipped cream
Grated chocolate,
   to decorate
Chocolate-coated coffee
   beans, to decorate

1 Pour the rum and coffee into an Irish coffee cup. Sweeten to taste.

2 Float the whipped cream on top.

3 Garnish with grated chocolate and chocolate-coated coffee beans and serve.

Variations: Substitute Kahlúa for the dark rum, if you like.

BLACKJACK

makes 1

2 tablespoons Kirsch
60 ml (2 fl oz) fresh coffee
2 teaspoons brandy
Coffee granules,
   to decorate

1 Stir all the ingredients with crushed ice in a mixing glass, strain, then pour into a cocktail glass.

2 Serve garnished with coffee granules.

Variations:
Make a Roulette by substituting vodka for the Kirsch, if you like.

CAFÉ OSCAR

makes 1

1 tablespoon Kahlúa
1 tablespoon
    Amaretto di Galliano
hot coffee
double (heavy) cream
1 scoop vanilla ice cream

1 Pour the spirits into a glass, then top up with coffee.

2 Float the cream on top. Garnish with the ice cream.

Variation:
Make a Café Maria by substituting Tia Maria and Galliano for the Kahlúa and Amaretto.

IRISH COFFEE

makes 1

1 teaspoon brown sugar
2 tablespoons Baileys
    Irish Cream
hot black coffee
2 tablespoons fresh
    whipped cream
chocolate flakes or
    chocolate powder,
    to decorate

1 Stir the sugar into the Baileys. Top up with coffee. Float the fresh cream on top, then decorate with chocolate.

Variations:
Make Irish coffee by substituting a good Irish whisky such as Tullamore Dew or Jameson's for the Baileys.

Other liqueur coffees are:
French, with brandy,
English, with gin,
Russian, with vodka,
American, with Bourbon,
Calypso, with dark rum,
Jamaican, with Tia Maria,
Parisienne, with Grand Marnier,
Mexican, with Kahlúa,
Scottish, with Scotch,
Canadian, with rye.

COFFEE BREAK

makes 1

125 ml (4 fl oz) hot
    black coffee
1 tablespoon brandy
1 tablespoon Kahlúa
3 tablespoons
    whipped cream
1 maraschino cherry

1 Combine the coffee and liquors in an Irish coffee cup. Sweeten to taste.

2 Float the whipped cream on top. Garnish with a maraschino cherry and serve.

Variations:
Make a Peppermint Break by substituting crème de menthe for brandy.

COFFEE NUDGE

makes 1

2 teaspoons dark crème
    de cacao
2 teaspoons Kahlúa
1 tablespoon brandy
250 ml (8 fl oz) hot coffee
60 ml (2 fl oz)
    whipped cream

1 Combine the liqueurs and coffee. Top with whipped cream.

Variations:
Make Liquorice Coffee by substituting black sambuca for the brandy and coffee liqueur.

ICED ALCOHOLIC CAPPUCCINO

makes 1

90 ml (3 fl oz)
  strong espresso
60 ml (2 fl oz) milk
2 tablespoons vanilla syrup
1 tablespoon Kahlúa
1 tablespoon caramel syrup
60 ml (2 fl oz) cream

1 Blend all the ingredients with 2 scoops of ice.
Serve in a hurricane glass or snifter.

GALLIANO HOTSHOT

makes 1

2 tablespoons Galliano
2 tablespoons hot coffee
1 tablespoon double
    (heavy) cream

1   Pour the Galliano into a shot glass, then carefully pour the coffee on top. Finally, gently spoon the cream on top of the coffee layer.

ROYALE COFFEE

makes 1

2 tablespoons Cognac
150 ml (¼ pint) hot
    black coffee
3 tablespoons
    whipped cream
1 teaspoon grated chocolate

1 Add the coffee and Cognac to an Irish coffee cup and sweeten to taste. Gently float the whipped cream on top, sprinkle with chocolate and serve.

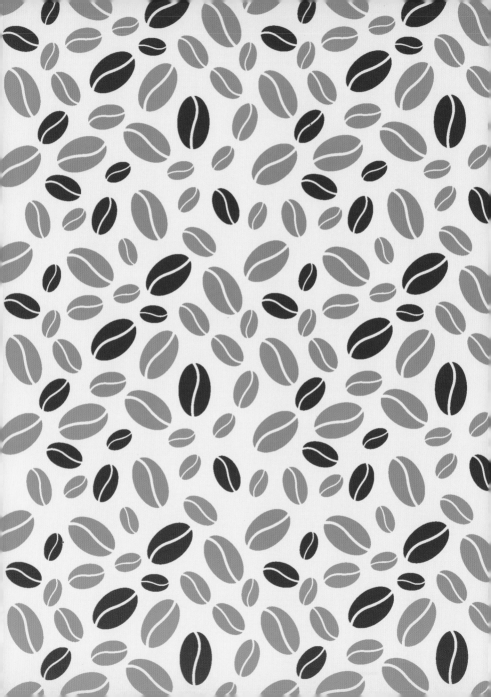

COFFEE COOKIES

MOCHA MERINGUES

makes 12

4 egg whites
1 cup superfine sugar
¼ teaspoon cream
   of tartar
1 tablespoon unsweetened
   cocoa powder
¼ teaspoon vanilla extract
¼ teaspoon instant coffee

1 Preheat the oven to 107°C/350°F. Line 2 baking sheets with parchment paper.

2 In a bowl, beat the egg whites and cream of tartar at high speed using an electric whisk, until soft peaks form. Gradually add the sugar, vanilla, cocoa and coffee.

3 Drop the mixture onto the prepared baking sheet in 12 dollops, about 2 inches apart.

4 Bake an hour or until firm. Turn off oven and let meringues cool in the oven for 1 hour. Do not open the oven door while the meringues cool.

COFFEE CHOC CHUNK COOKIES

makes 18

9 tablespoons butter
½ cup superfine sugar
⅓ cup brown sugar,
    firmly packed
1 tablespoon instant coffee
1 egg
1 ½ cups self-raising
    (self-rising) flour
1 cup chocolate chips

1 Preheat the oven to 180°C/350°F. Line 2 baking sheets with parchment paper.

2 In a bowl cream the butter and sugars. Beat in the coffee, then the egg.

3 Stir in the flour and chocolate chips.

4 Drop spoonfuls of the mixture onto the prepared baking sheets and bake for 10–15 minutes. Leave to stand for 10 minutes, before turning out onto a wire rack to cool.

COFFEE KISSES

makes 25

1 cup butter,
   at room temperature
½ cup powdered sugar,
   sifted, plus extra
   for dusting
2 teaspoons instant coffee,
   dissolved in
   1 tablespoon hot water,
   then cooled
1 cup flour, sifted
3 tablespoons dark
   (bittersweet) chocolate,
   melted

1 Preheat the oven to 180°C/350°F. Line 2 baking sheets with parchment paper.

2 In a bowl, beat the butter and powdered sugar until light and fluffy. Stir in the coffee and flour.

3 Spoon the mixture into a piping bag fitted with a medium star nozzle and pipe ¾ in rounds of mixture ¾ in apart on the prepared baking sheets.

4 Bake for 10–12 minutes, or until lightly browned. Leave to set for 5 minutes before turning out onto wire racks to cool completely.

5 Sandwich the cookies together with a little melted chocolate, then dust with powdered sugar.

Note:
These coffee cookies have a similar texture to shortbread, making the dough perfect for piping. For something different, pipe 5 cm (2 in) lengths instead of rounds. Rather than sandwiching the cookies together with chocolate, you may prefer to leave them plain and simply dust with powdered sugar.

CHOCOLATE MELTING MOMENTS

makes 13 pairs

1 cup butter, softened
⅔ cup powdered sugar
1 teaspoon vanilla extract
⅓ cup cornstarch
¼ cup unsweetened
   cocoa powder

1 Preheat the oven to 180°C/ 350°F. Line 2 baking sheets with parchment paper.

2 In a bowl, beat the butter and sugar together until fluffy.

3 Add the vanilla. Sift in the flour, cocoa and cornstarch and mix with a wooden spoon. Refrigerate for 1 hour.

4 Drop tablespoons of the mixture on to the prepared baking sheets. Flatten with a fork.

5 Bake for 10-13 minutes. Leave the cookies on the sheet for a few minutes, then let cool completely on a wire rack.

CHOCOLATE CREAM

8 tablespoons butter,
   softened
1 cup powdered sugar
1 teaspoon instant coffee
½ tablespoon
   unsweetened cocoa powder
2 tablespoons milk
1 teaspoon vanilla

1 Beat the butter in a bowl; beat in the remaining ingredients until smooth and easy to spread. Use to sandwich pairs of cookies together.

COFFEE PECAN COOKIES

makes 30

8 ¾ tablespoons butter,
    at room temperature
½ cup superfine sugar
½ teaspoon vanilla extract
1 egg
2 teaspoons instant coffee
1 ¾ cups plain
    (all-purpose) flour
1 teaspoon baking powder
1 tablespoon milk
2 cups pecans,
    finely chopped

1 In the bowl of an electric mixer, beat the butter, sugar and vanilla until pale and creamy. Add the egg and coffee and mix until well combined.

2 Sift the flour and baking powder over the butter mixture. Add the milk and stir until just combined. Divide the dough in half.

3 Roll each piece of dough into a 4.5 cm (1¾ in) diameter log. Roll the logs in the chopped pecans until well coated. Wrap each log in plastic wrap. Refrigerate for at least 30 minutes, or until firm.

4 Preheat the oven to 180°C/350°F. Line 2 baking sheets with parchment paper.

5 Using a sharp knife, slice the logs into 1.5 cm (½ in) wide rounds. Arrange on the prepared baking sheets and bake for 15–18 minutes, or until light golden. Allow to cool for about 5 minutes, then transfer to wire racks to cool completely.

COFFEE ICING

¾ cup powdered sugar
1 tablespoon boiling water
1 tablespoon butter,
    at room temperature
2 teaspoons instant coffee

1 To make the coffee icing, sift the powdered sugar into a bowl. Combine the boiling water, butter and coffee in a separate bowl and stir until the coffee is dissolved. Add to the powdered sugar and stir until the mixture is smooth.

2 Drop 1 teaspoon of icing onto the centre of each biscuit. Top with a pecan. Allow the icing to set before serving.

CHOCOLATE BOURBONS

makes 14-16

4 ¼ tablespoons butter,
   plus extra for greasing
¼ cup superfine sugar
1 tablespoon light corn syrup
1 cup plain (all-purpose) flour,
   plus extra for dusting
2 tablespoons unsweetened
   cocoa powder
½ teaspoon baking soda

1 Preheat the oven to 160°C/325°F. Lightly grease a baking sheet. In a bowl, cream the butter and sugar together until light and fluffy, then beat in the syrup.

2 Sift in the flour, cocoa and baking soda, then work into the creamed mixture to make a stiff paste.

3 Knead well, and roll out on a lightly floured surface into an oblong about 0.5 cm (¼ in) thick. Place on the prepared baking sheet. Bake for 15–20 minutes.

4 Cut into fingers of equal width while still warm. Leave to set for a few minutes, before turning out onto a wire rack to cool completely.

FILLING

3 ½ tablespoons butter
¾ cup powdered
   sugar, sifted
1 tablespoon unsweetened
   cocoa powder
1 teaspoon instant coffee

1 Beat the butter in a bowl until soft. Add the sugar, cocoa, and coffee and beat until smooth. Sandwich the cooled fingers with a layer of filling in the middle.

BRAZILIAN COFFEE COOKIES

makes 24

7 tablespoons butter
½ cup packed
    brown sugar
½ cup superfine sugar
1 egg
1½ teaspoons vanilla extract
1 tablespoon milk
2 ¾ cups plain
    (all-purpose) flour
½ teaspoon salt
¼ teaspoon baking soda
¼ teaspoon baking powder
2 tablespoons instant coffee

1 Preheat the oven to 200°C/400°F. Line 2 baking sheets with parchment paper.

2 In a bowl, beat the butter, sugars, egg, vanilla and milk until fluffy.

3 In a separate bowl, sift the flour, salt, baking soda, baking powder and instant coffee. Add to the sugar mixture and mix thoroughly.

4 Shape the dough in 2 cm (¾ in) balls. Arrange 5 cm (2 in) apart on the prepared baking sheets.

5 Flatten to 1 cm (⅜ in) thick. Bake for 8–10 minutes, or until lightly browned.

MACADAMIA COCONUT SQUARES

makes 48

18 tablespoons butter,
plus extra for greasing
¾ cup brown sugar,
firmly packed
1 tablespoon instant coffee
¼ teaspoon ground cinnamon
¼ teaspoon salt
2 cups plain
(all-purpose) flour

1 Preheat the oven to 160°C/325°F. Lightly grease a 8½ x 13 in baking pan and set aside.

2 In a mixing bowl, beat the butter, sugar, coffee, cinnamon and salt until light and fluffy. Stir in the flour a little at a time, blending well after each addition.

3 Spread evenly in the prepared pan. Bake for 20 minutes. Cool in the pan on a wire rack for 15 minutes.

TOPPING

3 eggs
2 teaspoons vanilla extract
¾ cup brown sugar,
firmly packed
¼ teaspoon ground cinnamon
¼ teaspoon salt
2 cups dry
unsweetened coconut
2 cups macadamias,
toasted and chopped

1 Beat the eggs and vanilla with the sugar, cinnamon and salt in a large bowl. Stir in the coconut and macadamia nuts. Spread evenly over the cooled baked layer.

2 Bake for 40–50 minutes, or until golden brown and firm to the touch. Use a knife to loosen around the edges while warm.

3 Cool completely in the pan on a wire rack. Cut into squares.

CAPPUCCINO CRISPS

makes about 75

18 tablespoons unsalted butter
1 cup sugar
6 tablespoons unsweetened
    cocoa powder
¼ teaspoon ground cinnamon
1 egg
2 teaspoons instant coffee
1 teaspoon vanilla extract
2 cups plain
    (all-purpose) flour,
    plus extra for dusting

1 Preheat the oven to 190°C/375°F.

2 Beat the butter, sugar, cocoa and cinnamon in a large bowl until well combined, then beat in the egg.

3 Stir the instant coffee, vanilla and 1 teaspoon water in a cup to dissolve the coffee. Beat into the butter mixture.

4 Beat in the flour until just blended. Divide the dough in half, wrap and chill until firm.

5 Roll out the dough on a lightly floured surface to about 0. 5 cm (¼ in) thick. Stamp out cookies using a 7.5 cm (3 in) wide cookie cutter in your favorite shape and place 2.5 cm (1 in) apart on an ungreased baking sheet.

6 Bake for 8 minutes, or until crisp. Leave to set for a few minutes, then turn out on to a wire rack to cool.

ICING

2 ¼ cups powdered sugar
¼ cup hot milk
3 tablespoons butter
1 tablespoon light corn syrup
2 teaspoons instant coffee
1 teaspoon vanilla extract
1 teaspoon olive oil
¼ teaspoon salt

1 In a medium bowl, gradually stir the hot milk into the powdered sugar until smooth. Beat in the butter until blended, then mix in the remaining ingredients with 1 tablespoon hot water.

2 Spoon the icing into a piping bag, or create your own by spooning the icing into a plastic bag and clipping off one corner. Drizzle a zigzag pattern on to the cooled cookies.

CHOCOLATE COFFEE TUILES

makes 25

¾ cup superfine sugar
3 large egg whites
½ cup butter,
    melted and cooled to
    room temperature
1 teaspoon vanilla extract
½ cup flour
1 teaspoon instant coffee
1 tablespoon unsweetened
    cocoa powder

1 Preheat the oven to 175°C/350°F. Line 2 baking sheets with a non-stick mat or parchment paper and oil generously.

2 Sift together flour, instant coffee, and cocoa powder.

3 Whisk sugar, egg whites, and vanilla to combine, not aerate. Add sifted flour, cocoa, and coffee mixture and mix until combined. Refrigerate for 2 hours.

4 Drop small spoonfuls of the mixture on oiled baking sheets. Spread the mixture with the back of a spoon to a thin, even consistency. Bake 11 minutes or until edges are set.

5 Remove from oven and let rest for 30 seconds. With a metal spatula, gently pry the cookies off of the sheet while still warm. Drape over a wooden spoon handle or rolling pin to cool.

COFFEE COOKIES

makes 12 pairs

8 tablespoons butter
½ cup sugar
1 egg
1 teaspoon coffee extract
2 cups self-rising flour

1 Preheat the oven to 180°C/350°F. Line 2 baking sheets with parchment paper.

2 In a bowl, cream the butter and sugar until light and fluffy. Beat in the egg. Add the coffee extract and flour and combine well.

3 Roll into balls and flatten with a fork. Arrange on baking sheets, spacing them slightly apart.

4 Bake for 30 minutes. Leave to set for a few minutes, then turn out onto a wire rack to go cold.

COFFEE ICING

3 ½ tablespoons
    butter, softened
⅔ cup sugar
2 teaspoons instant coffee

1 Beat the butter, powdered sugar, and instant coffee together until smooth. Use the frosting to join the cookies together in sandwiches.

CHEWY COFFEE COOKIES

makes 25

8 tablespoons butter,
   at room temperature,
   plus extra for greasing
½ cup brown sugar
1 large egg, plus 1 yolk
2 tablespoons coffee liqueur
½ cup molasses
3 tablespoons instant coffee
2 ¼ cups plain
   (all-purpose) flour
1 teaspoon ground cinnamon
½ teaspoon ground cardamom
2 teaspoons baking soda
½ cup powdered
   sugar, sifted

1 Preheat the oven to 180°C/350°F. Lightly grease 3 baking sheets.

2 In a bowl, cream the butter and sugar until light and fluffy. Add the egg, extra yolk, liqueur and molasses, and beat together.

3 Sift the coffee, flour, spices and baking soda into the egg mixture and fold in gently.

4 Roll tablespoons of the mixture into balls, then roll each in the powdered sugar. Arrange on the prepared baking sheets and bake for 12–14 minutes.

5 Leave to set on the baking sheets for a few minutes before turning out onto a wire rack to cool.

PECAN COFFEE DRIZZLES

makes 20

5 teaspoons instant coffee
7 tablespoons unsalted butter,
    at room temperature,
    plus extra for greasing
½ cup brown sugar
1 egg, lightly beaten
2 ½ cup plain
    (all-purpose) flour
1 teaspoon baking powder
½ cup pecans,
    roughly chopped
½ cup milk chocolate
2 tablespoons powdered sugar

1 Preheat the oven to 180°C/350°F. Lightly grease 2 baking sheets.

2 Dissolve 4 teaspoons of the instant coffee in 1 tablespoon boiling water. Set aside to cool slightly.

3 Beat the butter and sugar together in a bowl until light and creamy. Beat in the egg. Add the flour, baking powder and coffee mixture, then work together with your hands until the dough is smooth. Refrigerate for 10 minutes.

4 Roll out half of the mixture between two sheets of baking paper to 5 mm (¼ in) thick. Stamp out rounds using a 6 cm (2½ in) cookie cutter. Repeat with the remaining dough.

5 Place the cookies on the prepared baking sheets and bake for 10 minutes. Turn out on to a wire rack and scatter with nuts.

6 Melt the chocolate. Stir in the remaining coffee and the icing sugar and stir to combine. Drizzle over the cooled cookies. Leave to set.

COFFEE AND GINGER BISCOTTI

makes 40

Oil, for greasing
1 cup plain
    (all-purpose) flour
2 teaspoons ground coffee
3 egg whites
½ cup superfine sugar
½ cup unsalted
    almonds or hazelnuts
⅓ cup glacé ginger,
    finely diced

1 Preheat the oven to 160°C/325°F. Lightly grease a 1 lb loaf pan.

2 Sift the flour and coffee together in a bowl.

3 In a separate bowl, whisk the egg whites until soft peaks form. Gradually beat in the sugar. Continue beating until the sugar dissolves. Fold in the flour mixture. Fold in the nuts and ginger.

4 Spoon the batter into the prepared pan. Bake for 35 minutes. Leave to stand on a wire rack until completely cool. When cold, remove the bread from the pan. Wrap in aluminium foil. Store in a cool place for 2–3 days.

5 Preheat the oven to 120°C/250°F. Using a very sharp serrated or electric knife, cut the cooked loaf into wafer-thin slices. Arrange on ungreased baking sheets. Bake for 45–60 minutes or until dry and crisp.

Note:
You could swap the hazelnuts or almonds and ginger for any whole nut or dried fruit and spice that you prefer. For something festive, try cherries, citrus zest, and Brazil nuts, or use pistachios, glacé pears, and ground cardamom.

COFFEE
CUPCAKES

FRENCH COFFEE CUPCAKES

makes 12

9 tablespoons butter
¼ cup milk
2 tablespoons powdered milk
1 tablespoon instant coffee
2 eggs
1 cup superfine sugar
1 ¾ cups self-rising flour
¼ cup Grand Marnier

1 Preheat the oven to 180°C/350°F. Line a 12-cup muffin tin with paper liners.

2 In a saucepan, heat the butter, milk, powdered milk and coffee gently and stir until the butter is melted. Allow to cool.

3 In a large bowl, whisk the eggs with an electric mixer until thick and creamy. Add the sugar gradually, then stir in half the butter mixture and half the flour and beat well. Add the Grand Marnier, then the remaining butter mixture and flour and beat until smooth.

4 Divide the batter evenly between the paper liners. Bake for 20 minutes until risen and firm to the touch. Allow to cool for a few minutes and then transfer to a wire rack. Allow to cool completely before icing.

TOPPING

1 ½ cups powdered sugar
½ cup powdered milk
9 tablespoons butter,
    softened
1 tablespoon Grand Marnier
candied orange zest,
    to decorate

1 Combine all of the ingredients except the Grand Marnier in a medium bowl and beat with an electric mixer on low speed for 1 minute. Increase the speed and beat until light and fluffy. Slowly add the Grand Marnier and mix until thoroughly combined.

2 Half-fill a piping bag fitted with a nozzle with the mixture and pipe onto all cupcakes. Decorate with orange zest.

LONG MACCHIATO CUPCAKES

makes 12

1 cup plain (all-purpose) flour
1 ¾ cup self-rising flour
9 tablespoons butter,
    softened
¼ teaspoon vanilla extract
1 cup superfine sugar
2 eggs
½ cup instant coffee
¾ cup water

1 Preheat the oven to 180°C/350°F. Line a 12-cup muffin tin with paper liners.

2 Sift the dry ingredients together into a bowl.

3 In another medium bowl, beat the butter, vanilla and sugar with an electric mixer until creamy. Add the eggs one at a time and beat until well combined. Stir in the coffee.

4 Add the dry ingredients to the butter mixture and combine thoroughly, then slowly add the water and mix again.

5 Divide the mixture evenly between the paper liners. Bake for approximately 20 minutes until risen and firm to the touch. Allow to cool for a few minutes and then transfer to a wire rack. Allow to cool completely before icing.

TOPPING

1 ¾ cup powdered sugar
1 ¾ cup powdered milk
7 tablespoons butter,
    softened
¼ cup milk
4 drops vanilla extract
1 tablespoon instant coffee

1 Combine all of the ingredients except for the instant coffee in a medium bowl and beat with an electric mixer for 1 minute. Turn the speed up and beat again.

2 Add 1 teaspoon of water to the instant coffee and add to the topping, stirring only once. Spread the topping evenly onto the cupcakes.

COFFEE ALMOND CUPCAKES

makes 12

9 teaspoons butter,
   softened
1 cup superfine sugar
2 eggs, lightly beaten
¾ cup milk
1 ⅔ cup self-rising flour
¼ teaspoon baking powder
½ cup ground almonds
   or almond meal
½ cup unsweetened
   cocoa powder
¼ teaspoon instant coffee
½ cup slivered almonds

1 Preheat oven to 175°C/350°F. Line a 12-cup muffin tin with paper liners.

2 In a medium bowl, beat together the butter and sugar until light and fluffy. Mix in beaten eggs.

3 Add the milk and flour and stir to combine. Add the remaining ingredients. Mix with a wooden spoon for 2 minutes, until light and creamy.

4 Divide the batter evenly between the paper liners. Bake for 18-20 minutes, until risen and firm to the touch. Transfer to a wire rack to cool completely before icing.

TOPPING

8 tablespoons butter
1 cup powdered sugar
1 teaspoon almond extract
1 teaspoon instant coffee
36 chocolate balls,
   to decorate

1 Combine all of the topping ingredients except for the chocolate balls in a small bowl and mix well, until smooth and easy to spread. Spoon onto cupcakes and decorate each cake with the chocolate balls.

LONG BLACK CUPCAKES

makes 12

2 ¾ cup self-rising flour
1 ⅓ cup plain
    (all-purpose) flour
½ cup unsweetened
    cocoa powder
¾ cup butter, softened
1 ⅓ cup caster
    (superfine) sugar
3 eggs
¼ cup instant coffee
1 cup water

1 Preheat the oven to 180°C/350°F. Line a 12-cup muffin tin with paper liners.

2 Sift the flours and cocoa powder together into a bowl.

3 In another bowl, beat the butter and sugar until creamy. Add the eggs, one at a time, and beat until well combined. Stir in the coffee.

4 Add the dry ingredients to the butter mixture and combine thoroughly, then slowly add the water and mix again.

5 Divide the batter evenly between the paper liners. Bake for 20 minutes, or until risen and firm to the touch. Allow to cool for a few minutes and then transfer to a wire rack. Allow to cool completely before icing.

TOPPING

1 tablespoon instant coffee
¾ cup heavy cream
2 cups dark (bittersweet)
    chocolate, finely chopped

1 Meanwhile, heat the coffee and cream gently in a saucepan. Pour the mixture over the chocolate to melt it, and stir thoroughly. Let cool. Tip the mixture into a piping bag fitted with a star-shaped nozzle and pipe onto all cupcakes.

COFFEE AND HAZELNUT CAKES

makes 12

9 tablespoons butter
½ cup milk
2 teaspoons instant coffee
2 eggs
1 cup superfine sugar
1 ¾ cups self-rising flour
½ cup chopped hazelnuts

1 Preheat the oven to 180°C/350°F. Line a 12-cup muffin tin with paper liners.

2 In a saucepan, heat the butter, milk and coffee gently and stir until the butter is melted. Allow to cool.

3 In a large bowl, whisk the eggs with an electric mixer until thick and creamy. Add the sugar gradually, then stir in half the butter mixture and half the flour and beat. Add the remaining butter mixture and flour and beat until smooth.

4 Divide the batter evenly between the paper liners. Bake for 20 minutes until risen and firm to the touch. Allow to cool for a few minutes and then transfer to a wire rack. Allow to cool completely before icing.

TOPPING

1 ⅓ cup powdered sugar
2 tablespoons instant coffee
9 tablespoons butter, softened
½ teaspoon vanilla extract
toasted hazelnuts,
    chopped, to decorate
powdered sugar and
    unsweetened cocoa
    powder, for dusting

1 While the cupcakes cool, combine all of the ingredients in a medium bowl and beat slowly with an electric mixer for 1 minute. Turn up the speed and beat until light and fluffy.

2 Half-fill a piping bag fitted with a nozzle and pipe topping onto the cupcakes. Scatter with hazelnuts and dust with icing sugar and cocoa powder.

PECAN COFFEE CRUNCH CUPCAKES

makes 12

8 tablespoons butter,
    softened
1 cup superfine sugar
3 eggs, lightly beaten
¼ cup milk
1 ½ cup self-rising flour,
    sifted
1 tablespoon espresso coffee
½ cup pecans, chopped
1 tablespoon light corn syrup

1 Preheat the oven to 160°C/320°F. Line a 12-cup muffin tin with paper liners.

2 In a medium bowl, beat the butter and sugar until light and fluffy, then mix in the beaten eggs.

3 Add the milk and flour, and beat to combine. Add the remaining ingredients. Mix with a wooden spoon for 2 minutes or until it is until light and creamy.

4 Divide the batter evenly between the paper liners. Bake for 18–20 minutes until risen and firm to the touch. Allow to cool for a few minutes, then transfer to a wire rack. Allow to cool completely before adding the topping.

TOPPING

1 cup brown sugar,
    firmly packed
5 ¼ tablespoon
    unsalted butter
1 tablespoon water
1 teaspoon vanilla extract
1 cup pecans

1 Combine the sugar, butter, water and vanilla in a saucepan. Bring to a simmer over medium-low heat, stirring constantly. Allow to simmer for 1 minute without stirring. Remove from heat and add the pecans. Allow the topping to cool slightly before spooning it on to the cakes in mounds.

MOCHA CHOC CHIP CUPCAKES

makes 12

2 eggs, lightly beaten
9 tablespoons butter,
    softened
1 cup superfine sugar
½ cup milk
2 cups self-rising flour
2 tablespoons
    freshly ground coffee
½ cup mini chocolate chips

1 Preheat the oven to 160°C/320°F. Line a 12-cup muffin tin with paper liners.

2 In a medium bowl, lightly beat the eggs, butter and sugar, then mix until light and fluffy.

3 Add the milk, flour and ground coffee, and stir to combine. Beat until light and fluffy. Stir in the chocolate chips.

4 Divide the batter between the paper liners. Bake for 18–20 minutes until risen and firm to the touch. Cool for a few minutes, then transfer to a wire rack to cool completely.

TOPPING

1 ⅓ cup sugar
9 tablespoons butter,
    softened
1 teaspoon ground coffee
mini chocolate chips,
    to decorate

1 Mix together the powdered sugar, butter and coffee until well combined, then beat until light and fluffy. Use a piping bag fitted with a star nozzle to pipe the topping onto the cupcakes. Decorate with chocolate chips.

SPICED COFFEE CREAM CAKES

makes 12

9 tablespoons butter,
    softened
1 ¾ cup powdered sugar
2 eggs, lightly beaten
½ cup milk
1 ¾ cup self-rising flour
2 tablespoons coffee beans,
    very finely ground
1 teaspoon allspice

1 Preheat the oven to 180°C/ 350°F. Line a 12-cup muffin tin with paper liners.

2 In a medium bowl, beat the butter, powdered sugar and eggs until light and fluffy. Add the milk and flour and stir to combine. Add the remaining ingredients and mix well.

3 Divide the batter evenly between the paper liners. Bake for 15–20 minutes until risen and firm to the touch. Allow to cool for a few minutes and then transfer to a wire rack. Allow to cool completely before icing.

TOPPING

4 cups whipped cream
allspice, for dusting

1 Spoon whipped cream on top of each cupcake and dust with allspice.

COFFEE WALNUT CUPCAKES

makes 12

9 tablespoons butter,
    softened
1 cup superfine sugar
1 tablespoon instant coffee
2 eggs, lightly beaten
2 cups self-rising flour
¼ cup chopped walnuts
½ cup milk

1 Preheat the oven to 200°C/ 400°F. Line a 12-cup muffin tin with paper liners.

2 In a medium bowl, beat the butter, sugar, and 2 teaspoons of the coffee in a large bowl until creamy. Add the eggs, a little at a time, until just blended. Fold in the dry ingredients and milk.

3 Divide the batter evenly between the paper liners. Bake for 12–15 minutes until risen and firm to the touch. Allow to cool for a few minutes and then transfer to a wire rack. Allow to cool completely before icing.

TOPPING

1 ¾ cup powdered sugar
12 whole walnut halves

1 Combine the powdered sugar and remaining coffee, and mix with just enough water to make a soft icing. Ice each cupcake and top each with a walnut half.

IRISH COFFEE CUPCAKES

makes 12

18 tablespoons butter,
   softened
1 cup milk
2 teaspoons powdered milk
¼ cup instant coffee
6 eggs
1 ¾ cup superfine sugar
2 ¾ cup self-rising flour
½ cup Irish whiskey

1 Preheat the oven to 180°C/350°F. Line a 12-cup muffin tin with paper liners. In a saucepan, heat the butter, milk, powdered milk and coffee gently and stir until butter is melted. Allow to cool.

2 In a large bowl, whisk the eggs with an electric mixer until thick and creamy. Add the sugar gradually, then stir in half the butter mixture and flour and beat. Add the whiskey and the remaining butter mixture and flour and beat until smooth.

3 Divide the batter evenly between the paper liners. Bake for 20 minutes until risen and firm to the touch. Allow to cool for a few minutes and then transfer to a wire rack. Allow to cool completely before icing.

TOPPING

2 ⅓ cup powdered sugar
1 ¾ cup powdered milk
7 tablespoons butter,
   softened
¼ cup milk
1 tablespoon
   Irish whiskey
shamrock sprinkles

1 Meanwhile, combine all the ingredients except for the whiskey and shamrocks in a medium bowl and beat with an electric mixer for 1 minute. Turn up the speed up and beat again. Add the whiskey slowly and mix again until thoroughly combined. Half-fill a piping bag fitted with a nozzle with the mixture and pipe onto all cupcakes. Scatter with the shamrocks.

HAZELNUT MOCHA CUPCAKES

makes 12

8 tablespoons butter,
    softened
1 cup superfine sugar
3 eggs, lightly beaten
½ cup milk
1 ⅔ cup self-rising flour,
    sifted
¼ teaspoon baking powder
½ cup ground hazelnuts
    (hazelnut meal)
½ cup hazelnuts, chopped
1 tablespoon unsweetened
    cocoa powder
1 teaspoon instant coffee

1 Preheat the oven to 160°C/320°F. Line a 12-cup muffin tin with paper liners.

2 In a medium bowl, beat the butter and sugar until light and fluffy, then mix in the beaten eggs.

3 Add the milk and flour, and stir to combine. Add the remaining cake ingredients. Beat with a wooden spoon for 2 minutes, until light and creamy.

4 Divide the batter evenly between the paper liners. Bake for 18–20 minutes until risen and firm to the touch. Allow to cool for a few minutes, and then transfer to a wire rack. Allow to cool completely before icing.

TOPPING

1 cup powdered sugar
8 tablespoons unsalted butter,
    softened
1 tablespoon hazelnut liqueur
1 teaspoon instant coffee
36 coffee beans

1 Meanwhile, combine all the topping ingredients except for the coffee beans in a small bowl. Mix with a wooden spoon until smooth and spreadable, then spoon an even amount onto each cupcake. Decorate each cake with a few coffee beans.

PECAN PRALINE CUPCAKES

makes 12

9 tablespoons butter,
 softened
1 cup superfine sugar
2 eggs, lightly beaten
½ cup milk
1 ⅔ cup self-rising flour,
 sifted
1 tablespoon espresso coffee
½ cup pecans, chopped
1 tablespoon light corn syrup

1 Preheat the oven to 160°C/320°F. Line a 12-cup muffin tin with paper liners.

2 In a medium bowl, beat the butter and sugar until light and fluffy, then mix in the beaten eggs. Add the milk and flour, and stir to combine. Add the remaining ingredients and mix with a wooden spoon for 2 minutes, until light and creamy.

3 Divide the batter evenly between the paper liners. Bake for 18–20 minutes until risen and firm to the touch. Allow to cool for a few minutes, then transfer to a wire rack. Allow to cool completely before icing.

TOPPING

1 cup sugar
9 tablespoons butter,
 softened
1 ⅓ cup powdered sugar
¾ cup pecans, chopped

1 To make the praline, combine the sugar, 1 tablespoon butter, and ½ cup water in a pain. Bring to a boil, stirring often, and simmer over medium heat until the mixture turns golden. Stir in the pecans and quickly pour onto a well-oiled baking sheet. Allow to cool and harden, then break into pieces.

2 In a bowl, beat together the icing sugar and remaining butter until light and fluffy. Use a piping bag fitted with a plain nozzle to pipe the icing onto the cupcakes. Decorate with praline pieces.

CAPPUCCINO CUPCAKES

makes 12

1 cup butter, softened
1 ½ cup milk
1 tablespoon instant coffee
6 eggs
1 ¾ cup superfine sugar
3 cups self-rising flour

1 Preheat the oven to 180°C/350°F. Line a 12-cup muffin tin with paper liners.

2 In a saucepan, gently heat the butter, milk and coffee and stir until the butter is melted. Allow to cool.

3 In a large bowl, whisk the eggs with an electric mixer until thick and creamy. Add the sugar gradually, then stir in half the butter mixture and half the flour and beat well. Add the remaining butter mixture and flour and beat until smooth.

4 Divide the batter evenly between the paper liners. Bake for 20 minutes until risen and firm to the touch. Allow to cool for a few minutes and then transfer to a wire rack. Allow to cool completely before icing.

TOPPING

2 ¾ cup powdered sugar
1 cup powdered milk
2 tablespoons instant coffee
½ cup butter, softened
¼ cup milk
½ teaspoon vanilla extract
powdered sugar and
    unsweetened cocoa
    powder, for dusting

1 Meanwhile, combine all of the ingredients in a medium bowl and beat until light and fluffy. Fill a piping bag fitted with a plain nozzle and pipe onto all cupcakes. Dust with powdered sugar and cocoa.

CAFÉ PARISIENNE CUPCAKES

makes 12

9 tablespoons butter,
    softened
1 tablespoon instant coffee
2 eggs
1 cup superfine sugar
2 cups self-rising flour
½ cup brandy

1 Preheat the oven to 180°C/350°F. Line a 12-cup muffin tin with paper liners.

2 In a saucepan, heat the butter and coffee gently, stirring until the butter is melted. Allow to cool.

3 In a large bowl, whisk the eggs with an electric mixer until thick and creamy. Add the sugar gradually, then stir in half the butter mixture and half the flour and beat well. Add the brandy and the remaining butter mixture and flour and beat until smooth.

4 Divide the batter evenly between the paper liners. Bake for 20 minutes until risen and firm to the touch. Allow to cool for a few minutes then transfer to a wire rack. Allow to cool completely before icing.

TOPPING

1 ⅓ cup powdered sugar
1 cup powdered milk
1 tablespoon instant coffee
8 tablespoons butter,
    softened
2 tablespoons milk
2 tablespoons brandy
instant coffee, for dusting

1 Meanwhile, combine all of the ingredients in a medium bowl and beat until light and fluffy.

2 Fill a piping bag fitted with a nozzle with the mixture and pipe onto all cupcakes. Dust with instant coffee.

ITALIAN COFFEE CUPCAKES

makes 12

9 tablespoons butter,
   softened
4½ teaspoon vanilla extract
½ cup milk,
   scalded then cooled
2 eggs
1 cup superfine sugar
2 cups self-rising flour
1½ tablespoons powdered milk
1 tablespoon instant coffee
2 tablespoons Amaretto

1 Preheat the oven to 180°C/350°F. Line a 12-cup muffin tin with paper liners.

2 In a pan, gently heat the butter, vanilla and 2 tablespoons of milk and stir until the butter is melted. Remove from the heat, stir in the remaining milk and allow to cool.

3 In a large bowl, whisk the eggs with an electric mixer until thick and creamy. Add the sugar gradually, then stir in half the butter mixture and half the flour and beat well. Add the remaining butter mixture, flour, powdered milk, coffee and Amaretto and beat until smooth.

4 Divide the batter evenly between the paper liners. Bake for 20 minutes until risen and firm to the touch. Allow to cool for a few minutes and then transfer to a wire rack. Allow to cool completely before icing.

TOPPING

1 ⅓ cup powdered sugar
1 cup powdered milk
1 tablespoon instant coffee
8 tablespoons butter,
   softened
2 tablespoons milk
2 tablespoons Amaretto
unsweetened cocoa powder,
   for dusting

1 Meanwhile, combine all of the ingredients in a medium bowl and beat until light and fluffy. Place mixture into a piping bag fitted with a nozzle and pipe onto the cupcakes. Dust with cocoa.

MEXICAN COFFEE CUPCAKES

makes 12

9 tablespoons butter,
    softened
1 cup superfine sugar
2 eggs, lightly beaten
2 cups self-rising flour
¼ cup unsweetened
    cocoa powder
2 tablespoons instant coffee
¼ cup milk
¼ cup Kahlúa

1 Preheat the oven to 180°C/350°F. Line a 12-cup muffin tin with paper liners.

2 In a medium bowl, beat the butter and sugar until light and creamy. Add the eggs and beat until well combined.

3 Sift the dry ingredients over the butter mixture and combine thoroughly, then slowly add the milk and Kahlúa and mix again.

4 Divide the batter evenly between the paper liners. Bake for approximately 20 minutes until risen and firm to the touch. Allow to cool for a few minutes and then transfer to a wire rack. Allow to cool completely before icing.

TOPPING

1 tablespoon instant coffee
¾ cup heavy cream
2 tablespoons Kahlúa
1 ¼ cup bittersweet
    chocolate, chopped

1 Meanwhile, heat the coffee, cream and Kahlúa in a pan over gentle heat. Add the chocolate, stirring until melted. Fill a piping bag fitted with a star-shaped nozzle with the frosting and pipe onto the cupcakes.

COFFEE RAISIN CUPCAKES

makes 24

¾ cup plain (all-purpose) flour
1 teaspoon baking powder
¼ cup raisins
8 tablespoons butter, softened
½ cup superfine sugar
1 tablespoon instant coffee
2 eggs, lightly beaten

1 Preheat the oven to 200°C/400°F. Set out 24 mini paper cupcake liners on a baking sheet.

2 Stir together the flour and baking powder in a medium-bowl. Add the raisins.

3 In another bowl, beat the butter, sugar, and 2 teaspoons of the coffee until creamy. Add the eggs until just blended. Fold in the dry ingredients.

4 Divide the batter evenly between the paper liners. Bake for 12–15 minutes until risen and firm to the touch. Allow to cool for a few minutes and then transfer to a wire rack. Allow to cool completely before icing.

TOPPING

1 cup powdered sugar
2–3 tablespoons boiling water

1 Combine the powdered sugar and remaining coffee, and mix with enough water to make a soft icing. Apply icing to each cupcake with a knife.

MORNING COFFEE CUPCAKES

makes 12

9 tablespoons butter,
   softened
1 cup superfine sugar
2 eggs, lightly beaten
2 cups self-rising flour
6 tablespoons strong coffee
¼ cup milk
¼ cup Amaretto

1 Preheat the oven to 180°C/350°F. Line a 12-cup muffin tin with paper liners.

2 In a medium bowl, beat the butter and sugar until light and creamy. Stir in the eggs and beat until well combined.

3 Sift in the flour, then add the coffee, milk and Amaretto. Stir to combine thoroughly.

4 Divide the batter evenly between the paper liners. Bake for approximately 20 minutes until risen and firm to the touch. Allow to cool for a few minutes and then transfer to a wire rack. Allow to cool completely before icing.

TOPPING

1 ⅓ cup powdered sugar
1 cup powdered milk
1 tablespoon instant coffee
7 tablespoons butter,
   softened
2 tablespoons milk

1 Meanwhile, combine all of the ingredients except for the instant coffee in a medium bowl and beat until light and fluffy. Add 1 teaspoon of water to the coffee and add to the topping, stirring only once. Spread evenly onto cupcakes.

COFFEE MUDS

makes 12

2 ½ cups chocolate
graham crackers
(about 15 cracker sheets)
1 cup butter, softened
1 ¼ cup (8 oz) dark
(bittersweet) chocolate
5 tablespoons light corn syrup
3 eggs, lightly beaten
1 tablespoon instant coffee

1 Preheat the oven to 180°C/350°F. Line a 12-cup muffin tin with paper liners.

2 Place the graham crackers into a plastic bag, seal, then crush with a rolling pin.

3 Melt 5 tablespoons of the butter in a pan. Remove from the heat and mix in the graham cracker crumbs. Divide the crumb mixture between the paper liners, pressing gently up the sides of each case. Refrigerate for 20 minutes, or until firm.

4 Put the remaining butter, chocolate and syrup into a heavy pan. Heat gently, stirring, until melted. Remove from the heat and cool for 5 minutes. Whisk in the eggs and coffee.

5 Spoon the batter over the graham cracker bases and bake for 18–20 minutes or until just firm to the touch. Leave to set for 5 minutes then transfer to a wire rack to cool.

TOPPING

¼ cup (1 ¾ oz) white
chocolate

1 Melt the white chocolate in a small bowl set over a pan of gently simmering water. Drizzle over the cakes.

COFFEE AND WALNUT SURPRISES

serves 12

1 cup butter,
    at room temperature
½ cup sugar
2 eggs
2 tablespoons Baileys
    Irish Cream
1 cup walnuts,
    chopped
2 tablespoons instant coffee
1 ½ cup self-rising flour

1 Preheat the oven to 180°C/350°F. Line the cups of a 12-cup muffin tin with paper liners.

2 In a bowl, beat the butter and sugar until light and fluffy. Stir in the eggs, Baileys and walnuts. Sift in the coffee and flour and mix to combine.

3 Divide the mixture evenly between the prepared paper liners.

4 Bake for 15–20 minutes, or until risen and firm.

5 Leave to set for 10 minutes, then turn out onto a wire rack to cool. Remove the paper liners.

SAUCE

1/2 cup superfine sugar
1 cup heavy cream
1 tablespoon instant coffee

1 Heat the sugar and ¼ cup water in saucepan until the mixture is boiling and the sugar dissolves. Reduce the heat, simmer until golden. Add the cream and coffee. Bring to a boil and simmer until the coffee dissolves and the sauce thickens. Pour over the cakes.

COFFEE CAKES

MOCHA DESSERT CAKE

serves 6-8

½ cup (3 ½ oz) chocolate
10 tablespoons butter,
    plus extra for greasing
1 cup superfine sugar
1 cup strong black coffee
1 cup all-purpose flour
4 tablespoons corn starch
1 egg

1. Preheat the oven to 160°C/325°F. Grease and line the base of an 8-inch round cake pan with baking paper.

2. Mix the chocolate, butter, sugar and coffee in a saucepan and heat gently until the butter and chocolate have melted and the mixture is smooth.

3. Remove from the heat. Sift in the flour and corn starch and add the egg. Beat with a wooden spoon until smooth, then pour the mixture into the cake pan.

4. Bake for 50–60 minutes, or until the cake is firm. Let stand in the cake pan for 10 minutes before turning onto a wire rack.

5. Serve dusted with cocoa powder and a dollop of whipped cream.

CAPPUCCINO CHEESECAKE

serves 12

CRUST

1 ¼ cup finely chopped nuts
(almonds, walnuts)
2 tablespoons sugar
3 ½ tablespoons butter,
melted

1 Preheat the oven to 160°C/325°F.

2 Thoroughly mix the nuts, sugar, and butter. Press the mixture into the base of a 9 inch springform pan. Bake for 10 minutes, remove from oven and allow to cool.

3 Increase the oven temperature to 230°C/450°F.

FILLING

4 ¼ cup (36 oz) cream cheese,
at room temperature
1 cup sugar
3 tablespoons
all-purpose flour
4 large eggs
1 cup sour cream
1 tablespoon instant coffee
¼ teaspoon ground cinnamon
Whipped cream,
for topping
Coffee beans,
to decorate

1 Combine the cream cheese, sugar and flour in the bowl of an electric mixer and mix on medium speed until well blended. Add the eggs, one at a time, mixing well after each addition. Blend in the sour cream.

2 Dissolve the coffee and cinnamon in ¼ cup boiling water. Cool, then gradually add to the cream cheese mixture, mixing until well blended. Pour over the base.

3 Bake for 10 minutes. Reduce the oven temperature to 120°C/250°F and continue baking for 1 hour.

4 Loosen the cake from the rim, allow to cool before removing. Chill. Serve topped with whipped cream and coffee beans.

COCOMO CHEESECAKE

serves 12

CRUST

1 cup finely-crushed
    graham crackers
3 tablespoons sugar
8 tablespoons butter,
    melted

1 Preheat the oven to 180°C/350°F.

2 Mix the graham cracker crumbs, sugar and butter thoroughly in a bowl. Press into the base of a 9 inch springform pan. Bake for 10 minutes.

FILLING

⅓ cup chocolate
3 tablespoons butter
2 cups (16 oz) cream cheese,
    at room temperature
1 ½ cup superfine sugar
5 large eggs
1 cup unsweetened
    shredded coconut

1 Melt the chocolate and butter over a low heat, stirring until smooth.

2 Combine the cream cheese and sugar in the bowl of an electric mixer, and mix on medium speed until well blended. Add the eggs one at a time, mixing well after each addition. Blend in the chocolate mixture and coconut, pour over the base.

3 Bake for 60 minutes or until set.

TOPPING

1 cup sour cream
2 tablespoons sugar
2 tablespoons
    passionfruit liqueur
1 teaspoon instant coffee
unsweetened cocoa powder,
    for dusting

1 To make the topping, combine the sour cream, sugar, liqueur and coffee in a large bowl, then spread over the cheesecake.

2 Reduce the oven temperature to 150°C/300°F and bake for 5 minutes.

3 Loosen the cake from the rim of the pan, and leave to cool before turning out. Chill and serve dusted with cocoa powder.

ESPRESSO CAKE

serves 8-10

¾ cup finely ground
  espresso coffee beans
1 cup butter,
  plus extra for greasing
1 ¼ cup sugar
3 eggs
1 tablespoon vanilla extract
1 ¾ cup all-purpose flour
3 teaspoons baking powder
1 teaspoon ground cinnamon

1 Preheat the oven to 180°C/350°F. Grease and line an 8 inch round cake pan with baking paper.

2 Pour 1 cup boiling water over half the ground coffee beans and leave to steep in a pitcher for 5 minutes.

3 Put the butter in a mixing bowl. Strain the liquid from the beans over the butter and stir until the butter melts. Discard the strained beans.

4 Mix in the sugar, eggs and vanilla and beat with a wooden spoon until combined. Sift the flour and baking powder into the mixture and mix in with the remaining ground coffee beans.

5 Pour the batter into the prepared cake tin. Bake for 50–55 minutes, or until the cake springs back when lightly touched.

6 Leave to set in the tin for 10 minutes before turning out onto a wire rack to go cold. Dust with cinnamon.

COFFEE CREAM

1 ¼ cup heavy cream
1 tablespoon powdered sugar
2 tablespoons strong-brewed
  espresso coffee

1 Whip the cream until soft, then beat in the powdered sugar and coffee. Serve with the cake.

COFFEE SANDWICH CAKE

serves 8

1 cup butter,
    at room temperature
1 cup superfine sugar
6 eggs, lightly beaten
2 cups self-rising flour,
    sifted

1 Preheat the oven to 160°C/325°F. Grease and line two 7 inch cake pans.

2 Beat the butter and sugar in a large bowl until light and fluffy. Add the eggs, one at a time and beat well. Sift over the flour and mix to combine.

3 Divide the batter between the prepared pans and bake for 30–35 minutes, or until golden. Leave to set in the pans for a few minutes then turn out onto a wire rack to cool.

FILLING

1 tablespoon coffee liqueur
½ cup heavy cream,
    whipped

1 Fold the liqueur into the whipped cream.

2 Spread the filling over one cake and top with the remaining cake.

ICING

4 ½ tablespoons butter,
    softened
⅔ cup powdered sugar,
    sifted
½ teaspoon ground cinnamon
2 teaspoons instant coffee
    dissolved in
    2 teaspoons hot water,
    then cooled

1 Beat the butter, powdered sugar, cinnamon and coffee in a large bowl until light and fluffy.

2 Spread the icing over the top of the cake.

COFFEE CHARLOTTE

serves 4

Oil, for greasing
½ cup raw sugar
1 egg
1 ¼ cup heavy cream,
    whipped
2 tablespoons instant coffee,
    dissolved in
    1 tablespoon water
¼ cup rum
12 lady fingers (savoiardi)
unsweetened cocoa powder,
    for dusting

1 Grease and line a square or rectangular baking pan with baking paper.

2 In a bowl, beat the sugar and egg until light and fluffy. Fold in the cream and coffee.

3 In a separate bowl, combine the rum with ½ cup water. Dip the lady fingers into the rum mixture, then arrange side by side in the base of the prepared baking pan.

4 Fill the pan with alternating layers of cream and lady fingers, ending with the lady fingers.

5 Refrigerate for 3 hours, then carefully turn out onto a serving plate. Dust with cocoa and serve.

CAPPUCCINO PIE

serves 4-6

BASE

2 ¼ cups chocolate
    graham crackers
    (about 12 cracker sheets)
3 ½ tablespoons butter,
    melted
1 tablespoon instant coffee

1 Preheat the oven to 190°C/375°F.

2 Finely crush the graham crackers. Pour in the melted butter, add the instant coffee and mix to combine. Press the mixture into the base of an 8 inch springform pan. Refrigerate.

FILLING

1 cup milk
2 tablespoons instant coffee
⅓ cup sugar
⅓ cup corn starch
2 egg yolks, beaten

1 Whisk the milk, coffee, sugar and corn starch together. Heat, stirring constantly, until the mixture boils and thickens. Remove from the heat and let cool completely.

2 Mix in the egg yolks. Pour into the prepared base.

TOPPING

2 egg whites
½ cup superfine sugar
½ teaspoon unsweetened
    cocoa powder
chocolate sticks,
    to decorate

1 Whisk the egg whites in a clean, grease-free bowl until stiff. Gradually beat in the sugar until the mixture is thick and glossy, then spread over the filling.

2 Bake for 10 minutes, or until just starting to colour. Dust with the cocoa and decorate with chocolate sticks.

COFFEE PECAN PIE

serves 8-10

5 tablespoons butter,
    plus extra for greasing
⅔ cup sugar
1 cup light corn syrup
3 eggs
1 cup pecans,
    coarsely chopped
1 teaspoon instant coffee,
    dissolved in
    1 teaspoon water
pinch of salt
1 cup semisweet
    chocolate chips
½ cup heavy cream
1 tablespoon powdered sugar
¼ teaspoon vanilla extract

1 Preheat the oven to 190°C/375°F. Grease a 8 ½ inch pie pan.

2 In a medium saucepan, melt the butter over a low heat. Stir in the sugar and light corn syrup and set aside to cool.

3 In a mixing bowl, beat the eggs. Stir in the chopped pecans, melted butter mixture and coffee.

4 Roll out the pastry between sheets of baking paper and use to line the pie pan.

5 Spread the chocolate chips evenly over the base of the pie crust.

6 Pour the pecan mixture over the top. Bake for 45–50 minutes, or until set. Let cool.

7 Cover and let stand at room temperature for about 8 hours before serving.

8 Whip the cream, icing sugar and vanilla together in a mixing bowl until stiff. Serve with the pie.

PASTRY

1 ⅓ cup all-purpose flour
8 ¾ tablespoons butter,
    chopped
¼ cup superfine sugar
1 egg yolk

1 To make the pie crust, combine the flour, butter and sugar in a food processor, and pulse until mixture resembles breadcrumbs.

2 Add the egg yolk and enough chilled water to form a dough. Knead lightly, wrap in plastic wrap and refrigerate for 30 minutes.

INDEX

Affogato agave 77
American 49

Babycino 71
Banana mocha milkshake 73
Blackjack 83
Brazilian coffee cookies 113

Café agave 79
Café Oscar 85
Café Parisienne cupcakes 157
Caffé latte 53
Cappuccino 59
Cappuccino cheesecake 175
Cappuccino crisps 117
Cappuccino cupcakes 155
Cappuccino pie 185
Caribbean coffee 81
Chewy coffee cookies 123
Chocolate bourbons 111
Chocolate coffee tuiles 119
Chocolate melting moments 107
Chocolate sauce 36
Cocomo cheesecake 177
Coffee, history of 6
    Art 27
    Arabica 11
    Barista 22
    Coffee blends 12

Coffee roasting 12
Creating the perfect espresso 10
Decaffeinated 14
Espresso machine 21
Fair Trade 15
Free-poured patterns 32
Grinding the beans 16
Macchina 21
Macinazione 16
Mano 22
Milk, pouring 32
    Heart 34
    Rosetta 35
Miscela 11
Organic 14
Patterns with
    chocolate 36
    Quick and simple 39
    Spider's web 38
Rainforest Alliance 15
Robusta 11
Shot length 45
Shot size 44
Storing 16
Which grind 18
Which grinder 16
    Blade grinders 17
    Burr grinders 17
Coffee almond cupcakes 135

Coffee and ginger biscotti 127
Coffee and hazelnut cakes 139
Coffee and walnut surprises 169
Coffee break 89
Coffee charlotte 183
Coffee choc chunk cookies 103
Coffee cookies 121
Coffee kisses 105
Coffee muds 167
Coffee nudge 91
Coffee pecan cookies 109
Coffee pecan pie 187
Coffee raisin cupcakes 163
Coffee sandwich cake 181
Coffee walnut cupcakes 147

Espresso 47
Espresso cake 179

Flat white 57
French coffee cupcakes 131

Galliano hotshot 95

Hazelnut Mocha cupcakes 151
Hot mocha chocolate 69

Iced alcoholic cappuccino 93
Iced chocolate 67

Iced coffee 65
Irish coffee 87
Irish coffee cupcakes 149
Italian coffee cupcakes 159
Italian hot chocolate 69

Long black 49
Long black cupcakes 137
Long macchiato cupcakes 133

Macadamia coconut squares 115
Macchiato 51
Mexican coffee cupcakes 161
Mocha 61
Mocha choc chip cupcakes 143
Mocha dessert cake 173
Mocha meringues 101
Morning coffee cupcakes 165

Pecan coffee crunch cupcakes 141
Pecan coffee drizzles 125
Pecan praline cupcakes 153
Piccolo latte 55

Royale coffee 97

Spiced coffee cream cakes 145

Vienna coffee 63

THE BARISTA'S BIBLE

ISBN: 978-1-58423-623-8
First published in the United States of America, April 2017 by Gingko Press

Gingko Press, Inc.
1321 5th Street
Berkeley, CA, 94710, USA
Email: books@gingkopress.com
www.gingkopress.com

First Published and Distributed in 2015 by
Tan Yang International Pte Ltd

50 Playfair Road, #07-02
Noel Building, Singapore 367995
Tel: +65 289 9208
Fax: +65 289 9108
enquiry@tanyangintl.com
www.tanyangintl.com

Editing US Edition: Christl Hansman, Amy Detrich
Managing Director: Fiona Schultz
Designer: Weiming Huang
Production Director: Olga Dementiev
Printer: Toppan Leefung Printing Ltd (China)